THE WAY TO EXCELLENCE

Also by Shama Viola

Books & Decks

Bral Talej Divination Cards

The Bral Talej Guide Book: *Magical Signs for Divination*

Online Courses

Seven Steps to Spiritual Freedom - From Self Awareness to Self Realization

Conscious Co-Creation

Explore, Experience, Expand into Love

Bral Talej Divination Level One

The Excellence Blueprint - A Guide to Personal and Professional Mastery

Sacred Products designed by Shama

Sacred Language Mandala Prayer Flags

Sacred Language Mandala Window Cling

Sacred Language Charms (silver)

Art Collages

THE WAY TO EXCELLENCE

A Guide to Personal and Professional Mastery

SHAMA VIOLA

SHOCO
PRESS

Praise for The Excellence Blueprint

I came across The Excellence Blueprint offering and immediately was hooked in to its alluring potential. Over the course of seven weeks, through exercises and deep introspection, hidden truths were revealed and real desires and direction were laid out before me. Each week, care was given to each participant, with meaningful direction and encouragement. I highly recommend this journey if you love self exploration, aha moments and are looking for real movement toward your true desires. It's powerful, fun and reaches deep in your soul.

Carole S.

This course created a beautiful and focused way for accelerating the manifestation of your desires. It deepened my learning about the difference between wants and desires, and it illuminated shadow aspects of myself that I was not previously aware of.

Angela S.

The course in Excellence opened up memories both in my professional and personal life. When you approach things with this "blueprint" you raise yourself to another level that enables you to achieve much more than you could without that blueprint.

Steve A.

The Excellence Blueprint is an invitation to pursue our highest potential and manifest our dreams. The steps outlined in the program are both practical and doable. If you're willing to put in the effort and do the necessary work, the results can be transformative and positively life-changing. Overall, this information will help guide you in the right direction.

Mrina A.

I feel very honored and privileged to have partaken in the Blueprint Excellence course. One that I would recommend to anyone who wants to understand a deeper meaning of themselves and their life experiences, with all of the qualities that Shama exudes in herself. I thoroughly enjoyed the journey, and so blessed to have this opportunity.

Anne-Marie T.

In my experience, the Excellence Blueprint was not a magic formula, nor did it offer ready-made answers to my questions. It was something far greater: a deep, transformative inner journey, joyful and creative. Through the illustration of its thematic elements, masterfully presented and distilled to their essence by Shama Viola, the perception began to align with the intentions and actions. The questions and exercises became mirrors through which the patterns of consciousness grew clearer, revealing the forces that either propel or obstruct the flow of energy, and consequently, the unfolding of events in life.

Iosif H.

Contents

This book is lovingly and gratefully dedicated to:

LAZARIS*, who first brought my attention to these powerful teachings.*

SHAKTI GAWAIN, *for being an amazing example of what living vulnerability with Excellence looked like.*

SHOCO, *for her steadfast presence, loyal friendship and unwavering support.*

NEREIDE, *for being willing to receive and welcome all that I have to offer her.*

Foreword

Dear Reader,

It has been a joy and an honor to witness the unfolding of this work.

Shama Viola is not only a dear friend but also someone I've had the privilege of working with since 2019, supporting her in sharing many of her teachings. But in the spring of 2024, something new began to emerge. I remember sitting with her one morning at her office as she spoke about a course she felt called to create—a process to guide people step by step into living with true excellence. The idea was clear, alive, and already taking form. Within weeks, she was speaking about it publicly. By the fall, she was leading the first seven week intensive with a small mentoring group. The response was immediate and powerful.

Since then, more people have walked through the process with her, and the results continue to speak for themselves. The work is transformative—practical, grounded, and deeply effective. Now, just over a year after that initial spark, the course has become this book.

There is something powerful about learning from someone who truly lives what they teach. You can feel the authenticity. You can see the results. Shama is one of those rare teachers who walks her talk. Whether she's planting in her garden, preparing a meal, planning a journey, guiding a group—or even writing this book—she brings the same intention, presence, and mastery to every action. Excellence is not something she only teaches; it is something she embodies.

This book is offered in two parts. In Part One, Shama shares her own personal journey through the steps of excellence, told through stories, reflections, and the real-life experiences that shaped her. In Part Two, she hands the journey over to you. You'll receive the teachings, tools, and exercises—the exact steps Shama has lived and taught—to guide you in cultivating excellence in your own life.

If you choose to walk this path with sincerity and commitment, I can promise you: it will transform you. These steps are more than a method—they are a practice. A way of turning your desires into reality with clarity, elegance, and soul. Whether your goal is small or great—preparing a meal, having a meaningful conversation, launching a project, or stepping into a major life transition—these tools will support you in doing it all with excellence.

This is a path toward greater presence and conscious living. A way to bring more awareness, focus, and fulfillment into your daily life.

Welcome to the journey.

~ Shoco Evanko

Part I

MY JOURNEY TOWARDS EXCELLENCE

"We are used to chasing success as the ultimate goal, not realizing that if we cultivated excellence instead, success would be inevitable."

~ Shama Viola

Introduction

Excellence is not a destination—it is a way of being. It is the continuous unfolding of our potential, a refining of our thoughts, desires and actions, to align with the highest version of ourselves. Excellence is the art of creating a life infused with meaning, purpose, creativity, and grace.

To walk this path, we need a framework—a structure to guide and support us. Whether we're building a house, planting a garden, or learning a language, success requires both clarity and discipline. Without a framework, we often waste energy on frustration and unnecessary effort. But with the right guidance, the journey becomes clearer, smoother, and more aligned with our true nature.

This book provides a clear pathway: a transformative journey through Seven Steps that take us to Excellence. These steps are designed to help us align our choices, intentions and actions, with our highest potential. Together, they form a roadmap for creating a life of purpose and integrity while nurturing our personal growth. Each chapter will explore one of these steps, weaving together stories and insights to help us embrace and integrate these principles into our life. For those who want to delve deeper there are lessons and exercises at the end of the book.

The path to Excellence begins with Desire, the first step, and the foundation of the entire process. Desire is the spark that ignites the flame of creation. It is the force that propels us forward and gives direction to our will. Recognizing what we truly want is essential, as it allows us to harness our creative potential and make the appropriate choices to successfully reach its manifestation. Desire is not about attachment or fear-based needs but about deeply connecting to what fulfills and motivates us. Without desire, there is no movement forward— it is the foundation of all growth and creation.

With desire awakened, the next step is Clear Intention. While desire identifies what we want, intention clarifies why we want it. Clear intention aligns our motivations with our values and ensures that our goals benefit not only ourselves but also those around us. By understanding the deeper purpose behind our desires, we gain confidence and authenticity, transforming dreams into actionable pursuits.

Once we are clear about what we want and why we want it, to proceed on our path to Excellence we must embrace Impeccability and Vision. Impeccability calls us to act with discipline, focus, and integrity, staying aligned with our goals even when distractions arise. It is our commitment to work with constancy and determination towards the manifestation of our vision. Vision, on the other hand, invites us to imagine the life we are creating, to see how our goals will enrich not only our lives but the world around us. Together, this integration of masculine and feminine elements creates a dynamic balance between practical effort and inspired imagination.

As we take action, we are invited to move with Elegance. Elegance is the art of achieving goals with ease, flow, and grace. It reminds us that struggle and resistance are unnecessary when we walk in truth, and trust in the process. By embracing elegance, the journey itself becomes joyful, allowing life to unfold naturally and effortlessly, like a river carving its way through the landscape.

The path to excellence is not without challenges, which is why Courage and Joy are essential companions. Courage gives us the strength to face fears, uncertainty, and setbacks with resilience. It reminds us that growth doesn't provide us with guarantees but requires stepping into the unknown. Joy, meanwhile, brings lightness and celebration to the process, transforming even small victories into moments of gratitude. Together, courage and joy help us persevere and find delight along the way.

To deepen our progress, we turn to Understanding and Wisdom. Understanding satisfies our intellect, giving us the clarity and insight to make informed decisions. This gives us a sense of security which makes us feel well grounded in what we are doing. Wisdom, however, transcends the intellect, connecting us to our higher self and a broader perspective. When understanding and wisdom work together, we harmonize the more masculine practical approach with the feminine intuitive one, ensuring that each step is guided by both knowledge and insight.

Finally, we arrive at Excellence, the culmination of the process. Excellence is not about perfection; it is about alignment—living in harmony with our deepest values and highest aspirations. It is the integration of desire, intention, purposeful action and vision, an elegant way to allow our courage and joy, understanding and wisdom to seamlessly express who we truly are.

Excellence is not a finish line—it is a way of life, a continuous practice of showing up as our best selves in all that we do. It asks that we look within, confront our fears, and commit to the process of growth. It is not always easy, but it is always worth it. Through this journey, we will discover that excellence is not just something we achieve—it is something we become.

As you embark on this journey, you will discover how these seven steps interconnect and build upon one another. Each chapter will guide you through a step, sharing personal stories, actionable practices, and transformative insights to help you navigate your own path to excellence. You'll learn how to align your actions with the deepest desires of your heart— and how to live with greater clarity, courage, ease, and creativity.

The journey to excellence begins now. Let us walk this path together and unlock the beauty, potential, and brilliance that reside within us.

The Great Void
rested in eternal, moving stillness,
experiencing Itself as pure, undivided Oneness—

Then—
a subtle shudder stirred...
a wave of vibration...
and a thought was born—
an idea... a dream... a question...

A spark of **DESIRE**
awakened and expanded within the Infinite—
a yearning to know Itself
through multiplicity and diversity,
through form and feeling,
through the illusion of separation and limitation.

And so, with **CLEAR INTENTION**,
Divine Mind burst forth infinite answers—
opening all possible paths,
creating worlds upon worlds,
an endless array of forms,
each a facet of the One,
each carrying the seed of remembrance,
each destined to walk its sacred path
and one day return home,
bearing the harvest of experience.

Guided by a luminous **VISION**,
the One **IMPECCABLY** divided Itself
into myriad fragments—
stretching beyond the known,
to taste the sweetness and sorrow of duality,
to witness the mystery from every possible point of view.

With **ELEGANCE**, It shaped contrast and color.
With **COURAGE**, It entered shadow and light.
With every breath of becoming,
It delighted in the **JOY** of unfolding.

Through eons of dreaming, discovering, and expanding,
Divine Mind deepened the **UNDERSTANDING**
of Its own vastness and complexity.

And within the sacred paradox
of living unity and separation,
It embraced a **WISDOM**
born from every choice and experience of Its creation.
And It knew—with peace and wonder—
that all was well.

And Its laughter echoed forth
with the radiance of **EXCELLENCE**...

"As above, so below..."

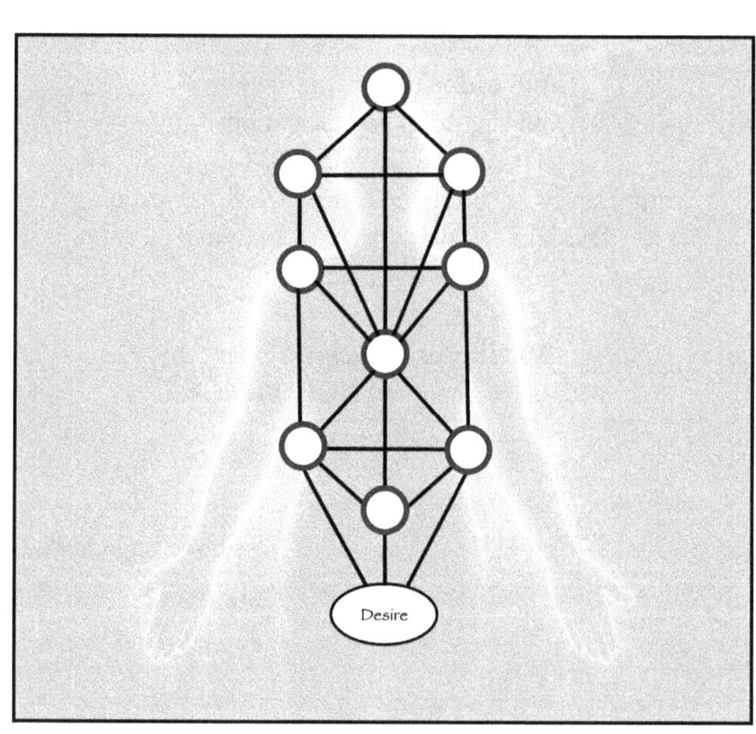

Desire

1

Awakening the Flame: Desire —The Spark of Creation

"The Promise of Next Year"

I was four years old when my mother died, and the world as I knew it collapsed in an instant.

Unable to care for me, my father brought me to an orphanage. Its large and silent halls were as intimidating as the black vestments of the nuns, the whole environment spoke of rigid rules and expected behavior. It felt like a cold and hollow replacement for the warmth of the home I had lost.

I felt confused, unable to speak and ask what was happening. Deep down after my father left me there, I remained convinced that he would come back for me. But he didn't.

Every year, he visited, and every year, he promised, "Next year, I'll bring you home." I clung to those words like a lifeline, but as the years passed, those promises became nothing more than shadows of hope that left me drowning in disappointment.

My childhood strategy for surviving in that environment was to dull all my emotions. I couldn't experience and express the sadness, the fear, the frustration, the anger, the disappointment I was hiding within. I knew that to feel safe obedience was required. And I needed numbness to do that. And so, I denied my feelings and used numbness as the strategy to cope with the life I was finding myself living.

For thirteen long years, my only desire was to return home. But the cycle of hope and heartbreak began to shape my relationship with desire, binding it to pain and disillusionment. I became afraid to want anything too passionately, fearing that it would only lead to more heartache.

When I finally left the orphanage at seventeen, life began to unfold in unexpected ways. Despite my fears, the universe seemed to meet me halfway. Jobs, relationships, and travel opportunities appeared as if by magic, each one guiding me closer to a life I hadn't dared to dream of. I cautiously allowed myself to want again—but always with restraint, never fully committing to my desires.

That pattern followed me into my twenties, until one day, something inside me shifted. At twenty-four, I made the boldest decision of my life: to leave Italy for America. At the time, I held a well-paid job in Bologna, the kind of position many would envy. But in my heart, I felt trapped. Italy, for all its beauty, felt like a cage, and the thought of settling into a predictable, conventional life was unbearable.

With my beloved cat in a wicker carrier and a single trunk of belongings shipped to a friend's address, I stepped onto a plane bound for the unknown. As the plane ascended, so did my resolve —I wasn't just leaving Italy, I was leaving behind the safe and predictable for a chance to finally live the life I had dared to dream of.

Within a week, I met a young man, fell in love, and soon found myself pregnant. Together, we left New York City for California, ready to embrace a free-spirited, bohemian lifestyle. For the first time, my deepest desires—for freedom, self-expression, and creativity—were no longer just ideas in my mind. They were my reality.

Looking back, I see now that embracing my deepest desires wasn't just about achieving a dream—it was about reclaiming the power to create my own reality. When we align with what we truly yearn for, life has a way of rising to meet us, transforming even the boldest dreams into lived experiences.

Desire: The Spark of Becoming

Desire, when embraced, becomes a river of energy. Left unchecked, it may scatter and lose focus. But when channeled with clarity and intention, it gains strength, carving paths through even the most resistant obstacles. As I've learned, the power of desire lies in its ability to awaken our creative potential—not by pushing harder, but by aligning with the truth of what we deeply yearn for.

When we honor our desires, we step into the role of creators rather than spectators. Aligned with our vision and purpose, we can forge a path of intentional growth, turning even the smallest step into a triumph of the soul.

Desire is where everything begins. It is the powerful fire within us—the force that stirs our soul and whispers, *there is more here for you.* Desire is not simply a wish; it is a current of life that calls us to awaken, to rise, and to move beyond the familiar into the realm of possibility. It is the ember that lights the flame of our aspirations, urging us forward into a fuller, richer expression of ourselves. Without it, there is no forward motion, no growth, no becoming.

Desire is always connected to **WILL** and **CHOICE**. These are the main elements needed to take **ACTION** towards realizing what we intend to achieve. They are what make desire powerful and not a mere fantasy. Will gives us the determination to stay the course, choice helps us align with our deepest intentions, and action bridges the gap between thought and creation.

Desire doesn't respond well to control. Control is a fear-based behavior that attempts to force outcomes according to our limited expectations. Desire, on the other hand, is a fire of creation that thrives on freedom and powerful expression. When combined with will, choice, and action, desire creates unexpected surprises, successful results, and personal fulfillment. Control, in contrast, leads to stress, rigid expectations, and anxiety—ultimately stifling the true potential of what desire can bring. When we pair desire with will and choice, and take courageous action, life has a way of responding in miraculous and unexpected ways.

"The Unexpected Gift"

Sometimes, life fulfills our deepest desires in ways we never expect. I learned this firsthand during one of the most idyllic chapters of my life—a time of comfort, success, and unexpected yearning. By 1979, both my husband and I were working for the legendary film director Francis Ford Coppola. What began as an exciting opportunity in San Francisco soon led to an invitation to move to his estate in Rutherford, nestled in the heart of Napa Valley. We settled into a charming cottage behind his villa, surrounded by vineyards and the rolling hills of wine country. It was a life many would envy: fulfilling work, beautiful surroundings, and a sense of security.

Yet, even in this paradise, a peculiar desire began to grow—a persistent, almost inexplicable yearning to spend ten days in Hawaii. At first, it was just a passing thought, but over time, it became a fixation. I could almost feel the warm sand beneath my feet and hear the waves crashing against the shore. The vision was so vivid, so real, that I became determined to make it happen.

Unfortunately, our finances didn't allow for such a luxury. Undeterred, I turned to an unconventional solution: sweepstakes. For an entire year, I scoured magazines, newspapers, and mailers for contests promising Hawaiian vacations. I poured my heart into each entry, imagining myself as the lucky winner every time I dropped another envelope in the mail. But despite my efforts, the dream stayed just out of reach.

Eventually, I had to let it go. Disappointment weighed heavily on me, but I couldn't keep pouring my energy into something that felt so unattainable. Slowly, the dream faded, and life moved on.

In 1986, after six fulfilling years with Coppola, I left my position, eager for a change. I took on an exciting role as a casting director for an independent film, and things looked good. Unfortunately, soon after the completion of this project, my marriage began to crumble. For months, I wrestled between the hope that it would get better and the pain of letting go, until one day, I knew I couldn't stay any longer. As I packed my belongings, uncertain of where life would take me next, the phone rang.

It was my dear friend Shakti Gawain. When I told her I was packing with no clear destination in mind, she didn't hesitate. *"Come stay with me at my condo in Belvedere,"* she said warmly. Her loving welcome and unwavering support were incredibly comforting. She then revealed to me that she was spending part of the year at her stunning estate in Kauai and invited me to join her there as well.

I was overwhelmed with disbelief and gratitude. For a moment, I couldn't speak. My heart raced as her words sank in. Kauai? I was going to Hawaii—not for ten days, but to live intermittently on the island! What had once seemed impossible was now unfolding effortlessly, in a way I never could have imagined.

That experience gave me more than just the fulfillment of a long-held dream. It brought me an incredible gift I hadn't dared to name: a best friend. For years, I had secretly yearned for a best friend, someone I could truly connect with at a profound level. While I had many friends and friendly relationships, I longed for that special bond. Through our shared experiences and unwavering support, Shakti and I formed an incredible friendship, a bond built on honesty, vulnerability, and shared joy—a connection that felt like home. In fulfilling my desire for Hawaii, life had given me something even greater, something that I had longed for in my heart forever: the unexpected gift of a deep friendship that enriched my life immeasurably.

Desire: The Trigger of Excitements and Fears

And yet, my relationship with desire has often been complex and fraught with confusion, mirroring my lack of understanding and appreciation for my own masculine energy—the part of me that takes bold action and pushes forward. The process of embracing my desires hasn't been easy. It has forced me to confront deeply held beliefs and conditioning: feelings of unworthiness, fear of failure or success, and distorted notions about spirituality, attachment, and renunciation. Each step in this process of owning up to my desires triggered resistance, numbness, and doubt, as well as a fear of disappointment that often kept me from taking risks.

For many of us, desire feels complicated, even perilous. It can bring up memories of yearning unmet, dreams dismissed, or the sting of judgment—those moments when wanting more seemed dangerous or foolish. To protect ourselves from disappointment, from the fear of being envied, judged, and abandoned, we bury our longing. We tell ourselves we're content, that we don't need much, that it's better to avoid the risk of failure or rejection. Yet, when we silence our desires, we also dim the very spark that propels us toward a vibrant life.

"The Cost of Hiding"

The first time I saw them, back in 1980, I felt both awe and intimidation, as well as a strong desire to be part of such a group.

A circle of powerful, confident women sat together, their energy magnetic and their bond undeniable. They were dedicated to overcoming weight issues, but to me, they represented so much more: strength, camaraderie, and a shared commitment to personal growth. I wanted so desperately to belong, but the voice of self-doubt whispered, "You're not like them, you are not 'enough'."

That voice had been with me for as long as I could remember. It told me I wasn't smart enough, strong enough, or worthy enough to claim a place among people like them. So instead of expressing the reason for my true desire to join their circle, I told them a lie—I joined under the pretense of wanting to lose weight, even though it wasn't a significant concern for me. I hoped that this façade would mask my inadequacies and win me a seat at the table.

But from the beginning, I lived in fear of being found out. This kept me in the shadows, hesitant to share, afraid to be seen. For months, I skirted the edges of the group, trying to be invisible, watching and listening but never truly engaging.

Then, one day, my turn came. All eyes turned to me, and I felt the walls close in. My heart raced, my throat tightened, and my mind went blank. Words seemed foreign; my voice locked away in fear. I wanted to disappear, to run from their powerful gazes and words, but I was frozen in place—paralyzed by the terror of finally being truly seen for what I was, a coward in their midst.

The session went on and on, everyone strongly sharing their feelings and opinions about my lack of authenticity and true participation. Unable to respond, in shock, I numbed myself out to be able to survive that confrontation. Ultimately, they told me to leave the group. I left in shame, feeling broken and exposed. I couldn't blame them; I hadn't been able to rise to the calling and meet them at their level. But the rejection hit me hard. I was left alone to confront the consequences of my dishonesty—not just with the group, but with myself.

In the weeks that followed, shame and self-doubt became my constant companions. I replayed the experience in my mind, trying to understand where I had gone wrong. Slowly, I began to see the truth: I had sabotaged myself by pretending to be something I wasn't. My fear of rejection had driven me to hide my real desires, and in doing so, I had denied myself the very connection I longed for.

Desire and its Denial

That painful experience taught me a hard but invaluable lesson. Hiding our true desires doesn't protect us—it isolates us. It keeps us from being seen, from being understood, and ultimately, from belonging. I realized that only by embracing my authenticity, by taking the risk of showing up as I truly was, I could begin to heal and reclaim my place in the world.

One of my most ingrained defense mechanisms against desire had been denial. Convincing myself that I didn't *really* want certain things, pretending instead to be content with what life put on my plate. This triggered a subtle sense of superiority, disguised as a virtue: *I've transcended material needs*, I'd tell myself. But in truth, this was only a shield to avoid confronting my deeper longings—a way to escape the vulnerability and fear of failure inherent to desiring.

True desire is not about grasping or clinging; it's the way our inner world reveals what we most need to express, experience, or create. Desire is a compass pointing us toward what matters most. It has nothing to do with greed or attachment—it is a deep recognition of the path that will bring us into greater wholeness and vitality.

"The Day I Turned Invisible"

When we are lost in denial, we're unconscious—blind to the misconceptions and distorted beliefs that quietly shape our choices. We don't realize the damage these patterns cause until something painful wakes us up. For me, that moment came on my 40th birthday.

That day, I sat alone in my bedroom, tears streaming down my face, wondering why I felt so unloved. It wasn't the kind of birthday I had imagined—because, in truth, what I had allowed myself to imagine was my own hidden fantasy, a true illusion.

A few weeks earlier, my husband and daughter had asked what I wanted to do for the occasion. A party? A dinner? Something special, just the three of us? But instead of expressing my true desires, I waved them off with a polite smile. "Nothing," I had said. "I don't care about birthdays—It's just another day." And every time they would bring up the topic, I would dismiss it as if it was the least important thing on earth for me.

I could see the confusion in their faces, but they respected my wishes. And so, when the day arrived, there was no cake, no celebration, no special gestures. Just an ordinary day that left me feeling hollow and forgotten.

By mid-afternoon, I was crying uncontrollably, consumed by a storm of disappointment and self-pity. I convinced myself that they didn't love me enough, that if they truly cared, they would have defied my wishes and thrown a surprise celebration. But beneath the surface of my anger and sadness was a truth I wasn't ready to face: I had done this to myself.

Deep down, I had wanted to be celebrated. I wanted my family to see me, to honor me, to make me feel special. But another part of me—the martyr part that had learned to suppress her own needs—had whispered that it was selfish to show or want such things. A good mother is supposed to be selfless, a good wife doesn't need attention. And so, I had said I wanted nothing, all the while hoping they would see through my words.

It wasn't until the tears subsided that the truth began to emerge. I had created this pain myself. By denying my desires, by pretending I didn't care, I had built the very loneliness I was now drowning in. That realization hit me hard: denying my needs didn't make me selfless—it made me a liar, someone who reveled in martyrdom, who wasn't taking responsibility for her own needs and desires but delegated to others her own happiness, while being filled with hidden resentment and drowning in self-pity.

That birthday taught me a hard but vital truth: when we silence our desires, we don't spare ourselves pain—we create it. To honor what we truly need and want is not selfish. It's an act of courage and authenticity, one that allows us to live fully and connect more deeply with those we love.

When we silence our desires, we don't just lose touch with what makes us come alive —we also lose touch with the people we love. My 40th birthday reminded me that expressing what we want isn't a selfish act; it's a bridge, a way of deepening connection and allowing others to see who we truly are, while giving them the chance to give to us. What's selfish is to always want to be in the role of the giver, feeling better than others who we relegate in the position of always be the takers. Suppressing desire doesn't protect us from pain; it creates a different kind of suffering—one built on misunderstanding and disconnection.

But desire cannot stand alone. To bring it into reality, we must engage all parts of ourselves: our thoughts, emotions, and actions. When these are aligned, desire moves from being a fleeting wish to a dynamic force of creation. Without alignment, we risk spinning in circles—thinking one thing, feeling another, and acting in yet another direction. But when we bring coherence to our being, desire becomes the wind at our back, driving us forward with clarity and grace.

And then, there is imagination—a partner to desire. Imagination allows us to dream freely, to envision what's possible, and to explore the steps that lead to fulfillment. It paints vivid pictures in our minds, awakening excitement and possibility. But imagination alone is not enough. We must also cultivate expectancy—a quiet but firm belief that what we long for is not just possible, but attainable. And as we lean into our desires, let us also bring lightness to the process. Humor and playfulness remind us to approach this journey with curiosity and joy, rather than fear or heaviness.

Desire: Embracing the Heartbeat of Creation

Speaking of fear—it often shadows our deepest desires, doesn't it? The fear of failure, of being judged, of change. Sometimes, fear arrives to slow us down, reminding us to move with care. Other times, in its effort to protect us, it whispers that our dreams are too big, too bold. But fear itself is not the enemy—*our fear of fear* is. Often without realizing it, we resist fear, believing it must be fought or hidden, lest it reveal our weaknesses. So, we judge it, deny it, suppress it... and in doing so, give it even more power.

When instead we meet it with compassion and curiosity, we uncover its deeper motivations. Fear is often a messenger. It needs our attention, not our avoidance. It can show us where we need more preparation, more patience, more healing—or simply more courage.

And when we truly listen, it can help us know whether we're ready to take the next step.

Finally, desire asks for clarity. What is it that we truly want? Why do we want it? Without clarity, our desires remain vague, elusive. But when we articulate them, when we name them, desire becomes a map, showing us the possible choices to make, the steps to take. A strong, clear desire fuels us when the journey feels long, when the challenges seem insurmountable. It keeps the flame alive.

Desire is not indulgent—it is essential. It is the red flame of vitality that burns within the root chakra, grounding us in the energy to create and expand. Like a flame that both warms and inspires, desire ignites the spark of possibility and reminds us that life is not merely something to endure, but something to embrace, shape, and celebrate with every fiber of our being.

So let us embrace desire—and even if fear or doubt emerge, let's consciously work to transform them into courage and joy. Let us allow desire to guide us into the extraordinary, to awaken our imaginations, and inspire our actions. For it is not only the first step on the path to excellence—it is the heartbeat of creation itself.

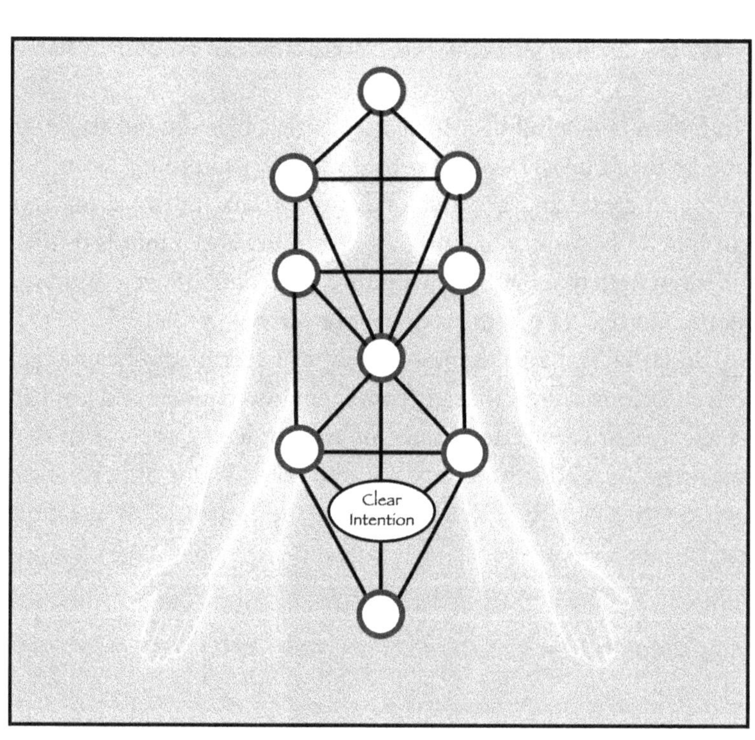

Clear
Intention

2

Clear Intention – A Cornerstone of Excellence

"A Promise Kept: The Power of Clear Intention"

Back in 1979—long before my time in Hawaii and before life began pulling my marriage in different directions—my husband and I were living in Marin County, California. He was working as Francis Ford Coppola's personal driver, and I was, unknowingly, on the cusp of a lesson that would shape how I understand the power of intention.

One evening, he came home with exciting news: the manager of Coppola's San Francisco mansion was leaving, and they were looking for a replacement. "You'd be perfect for this job," he said, urging me to apply.

The interview went well, and I felt confident I was the right fit. However, there was one complication: I had already promised my ten-year-old daughter a month-long trip to Italy. It was a promise I wasn't willing to break. When I explained my situation, they were disappointed but understanding and withdrew the offer.

I left the interview feeling calm and resolute. My heart was at peace. I felt deep within that the job was meant for me, yet my planned trip with my daughter came first. I didn't waver.

My daughter and I had a wonderful September in Italy! We

explored places from my childhood, visited new ones, and reconnected with old friends. It was a month full of joy, deep connection, and memories I still cherish.

When we returned, I wasn't surprised to learn that the job was still waiting for me. Despite their initial urgency, they had chosen to wait, believing, as I had, that I was the right person for the role.

This experience taught me that clear intention is not just about knowing what you want—it's about honoring your priorities and standing firm in your values. By trusting both,

I had found a way to "get my cake and eat it too."

From Desire to Clear Intention: Our Journey Continues

Once we have identified **WHAT** we desire, the next pivotal step on the path to excellence is clarifying our intention. By delving into the **WHY** behind our goal, we transition from a fleeting wish to a clear and resolute objective. This clarity infuses our desire with purpose and direction, making it easier to stay focused and impervious to distractions.

When we set clear intentions, we take an active role in shaping our reality. We ascend from passive observers to masterful creators, bringing our life into alignment with our deepest desires and values. This powerful practice paves the way for a simpler, more fulfilling, and profoundly meaningful existence.

The power of clear intention permeates every facet of our life. When we recognize our true motivations we shift from victimhood to empowerment. We seize control of our day, meeting challenges with resilience and a renewed sense of purpose.

When we embrace clear intention, we don't always see the entire path ahead. Sometimes the full understanding of "how" remains unclear but knowing why we choose that direction gives us a clarity of purpose that allows us to take the next step with confidence.

"A Leap of Faith: When Clear Intention Guides the Way"

After moving to Kauai in 1986, a new chapter began. Surrounded by nature and immersed in spiritual exploration, I felt as though I were living a dream—sharing precious time with my dear friend and renowned author Shakti Gawain, and deepening in the transformative consciousness work we both loved. The golden sands and lush green cliffs of the island became my sanctuary. Life had settled into a peaceful, fulfilling rhythm which lasted for a blessed few years.

Yet, in 1990, after a brief visit to Italy, a quiet but insistent longing began to stir within me.

It wasn't just nostalgia for my homeland—it was something deeper, a yearning to share the tools that had so profoundly changed my life. Voice Dialogue, a method that helps people access and integrate their inner selves, felt like a gift I was meant to bring to others. I wanted to return to Italy, to offer this work to those who, like me, might be seeking an evolutionary path to transformation.

Shakti, ever the supportive and protective friend, wasn't ready for me to leave. She pleaded with me to stay, worried that I was stepping away from something too precious to leave behind. But the pull was undeniable. My heart told me this was my path—I couldn't ignore it. So, with a mixture of hope, trepidation, and a head full of plans, I left my Kauai paradise a year later and returned to Italy, determined to follow my calling.

The first step was daunting. Translating the course materials into Italian was no small feat, especially after spending 25 years in the United States, where my native language had grown rusty. I retreated to a friend's remote mountain cabin, surrounded by stillness and solitude. For three months, I immersed myself in the task, driven by the clarity of my purpose. The days blurred into weeks, and I worked tirelessly, refining the translations and preparing the materials.

Yet, as my work progressed, the road ahead remained uncertain. My connections in Italy were few, and I had no idea where or how I would teach these courses. Still, I trusted my intention. I knew that the "how" would reveal itself when the time was right.

When the translations were complete, I decided to take a short vacation to recharge. I visited a Dutch colleague who was staying with a friend in Tuscany. Over lazy conversations, I shared my dream of bringing Voice Dialogue to Italy, confiding my uncertainty about how to begin.

What happened next felt like divine intervention.

After leaving them, I planned to spend a single night in Florence before traveling to Ferrara to visit my cousins. As I settled into my hotel room, the phone rang. A woman's voice, warm but hesitant, greeted me. She asked if she had reached the right person and quickly explained her story. She had recently discovered the Voice Dialogue book and felt drawn to learn more. Acting on impulse, she had called the contact number listed in the book, which turned out to belong to my Dutch colleague. He, in turn, had given her my name and the surprising detail of my hotel in Florence.

I was stunned. In a city of strangers, this woman had somehow found me—seeking the very knowledge I was so eager to share. It felt as though the universe had orchestrated this encounter, aligning the pieces with perfect timing.

A month later, thanks to this serendipitous connection, I was leading my first Voice Dialogue workshop in Florence. It was the beginning of a journey that would take me across Italy, sharing the work I loved with countless others.

Clear Intention Shapes Your Reality

This story is a testament to the power of desire and clarity of intention. While my three months of dedicated preparation laid the groundwork for success, it was my deep desire to contribute and my clear intention to bring this transformative work to Italy that truly paved the way. The entire process unfolded with remarkable grace and ease.

The power of clear intention was evident throughout. I was

certain of my purpose: to introduce the transformative tools of Voice Dialogue to Italy. That clarity guided my actions, and in time, the universe responded, aligning the right opportunities at the perfect moment.

Setting clear intentions is a powerful tool for shaping our reality. By consciously defining our goals and desires, and by clarifying the motivations behind them, we take an active role in creating a life that reflects our deepest values. This practice can lead to a simpler, fulfilling, and more meaningful existence.

When we approach life with clear intention, we are less likely to become victims of circumstances. Instead, we feel empowered and determined. While challenges may still arise, they no longer overwhelm us. We navigate them with confidence, knowing that we are on the right path.

Navigating Confusion

Clarity isn't always immediate, as I learned in moments of uncertainty. Sometimes, confusion precedes clarity, urging us to pause and reflect before taking the next step.

Often, we find ourselves lost in confusion, feeling unable to make decisions. This is also part of the process. Confusion arises when we haven't yet reached a place of clarity. It is there to slow us down, to make us reflect more deeply, and to allow us to better evaluate every aspect of the situation, including the consequences of our possible decisions.

Confusion is often uncomfortable, and we're not quick to welcome it. We judge ourselves for not feeling certain or in control, and we resist those unsettling "I don't know" moments. Yet confusion has a rightful place in our lives. If we can trust it, it becomes a quiet companion—offering pause, reflection, and the space for something deeper to emerge. In time, it can lead us to clarity. It slows us down just enough to ensure our choices are deliberate, conscious, and aligned when the moment to act arrives.

Clarity isn't always simple—it often requires us to confront our deepest doubts, fears, and insecurities. Sometimes, the journey to clear intention is as transformative as the destination itself.

"Love, Clarity, and the Courage to Trust"

My work in Italy had begun to flourish. Voice Dialogue was taking root, and I was leading workshops throughout the country. It was during this time—on a warm September afternoon in 1992—that I began teaching yet another course, one that would unexpectedly change the course of my life.

Among the participants was a young man whose enthusiasm and curiosity immediately stood out. Month after month, he returned, his interest in the work growing deeper with each session. By May 1993, after the weekend course had concluded, he asked to speak with me privately.

"I'm in love with you," he said, his voice steady but sincere.

I laughed, caught off guard but genuinely flattered. "That's very sweet," I replied, "but I'm not in love with you, nor am I open to any kind of relationship with a student."

He didn't flinch. Instead, he smiled softly and said, "I will wait."

Later that evening, I recounted the moment to my daughter, expecting her to laugh along with me at the absurdity of a 23-year-old professing love to her 49-year-old mother.

But instead of mockery, her response surprised me.

"Go for it! Why not? I would do it if I was your age." she said, her voice brimming with mischief and delight.

We laughed together, but her words lingered long after we hung up.

I had dismissed him outright, but as the days passed, I found myself thinking about him more and more. A week later, unable to resist, I picked up the phone under the pretense of thanking him for a thoughtful gift he'd given me that evening. The conversation flowed easily—too easily. His warmth and sincerity were disarming. Soon, our calls became a regular occurrence.

What followed was a period of intense confusion. My feelings were a whirlwind of doubt, fear, and longing. Could this really work? Was I making a terrible mistake? I wrestled with societal judgment and my own inner turmoil, questioning whether I should surrender to this unexpected love or protect myself from the risk of heartbreak. At times, the uncertainty was paralyzing. I didn't know whether to trust the growing connection or walk away from it altogether.

At first, the emotional turbulence felt overwhelming, but over time, something shifted. When I looked beyond the surface of my fears, I began to see the deeper purpose of this connection. Slowly, clarity emerged.

I realized that this love was a gift—an opportunity to experience growth, joy, and profound connection. It became clear that I wanted this, not because it was easy or free of challenges, but because it was true. I saw how this relationship was opening my heart in ways I hadn't thought possible, how it was bringing beauty, healing, and even a touch of magic into my life.

With trust, courage and surrender, I decided to embrace it fully, letting it transform us both. The love was so genuine and profound that we chose to marry. The seven years we shared were filled with adventure, learning, and mutual respect. When it was time for our journey as a couple to naturally end, it did so with grace and clarity, leaving behind not loss, but an enduring bond of love and gratitude.

In love, as in life, clear intention requires trust—not just in the outcome but in our ability to navigate the uncertainties along the way.

The Power and Art of Clear Intention

To fully harness the potential of our desires, we must cultivate a clear and purposeful intention. This requires understanding the profound *why* that drives us forward and allowing it to guide our actions with unwavering focus.

Clear intention is deeply connected to our emotions. It

reflects the reasons behind our choices and actions, and feelings are always part of the equation. Whether we choose out of fear or excitement, our emotions will be there when we set our intentions. Recognizing this connection helps us clarify what truly matters.

Like a compass, clear intention guides us through the complexities of life. It aligns our actions with our values and helps us navigate uncertainty with grace. When desire is coupled with clarity of purpose, extraordinary things can happen. Instead of reacting out of fear or habit, we begin creating a life that reflects our highest potential.

It's vital to ensure that our desires align with the highest good. This means thoughtfully considering the impact of our goals—not only on ourselves but also on our loved ones and the broader community. Intentions set with purity of purpose create a positive ripple effect, extending far beyond our own life.

By defining our goals and understanding why they matter, we step into an active role in shaping our reality. Challenges will undoubtedly arise, but with clear intention, we can meet them with confidence, knowing we are on the right path. This practice doesn't just transform our own lives—it can also inspire others to live with purpose and authenticity.

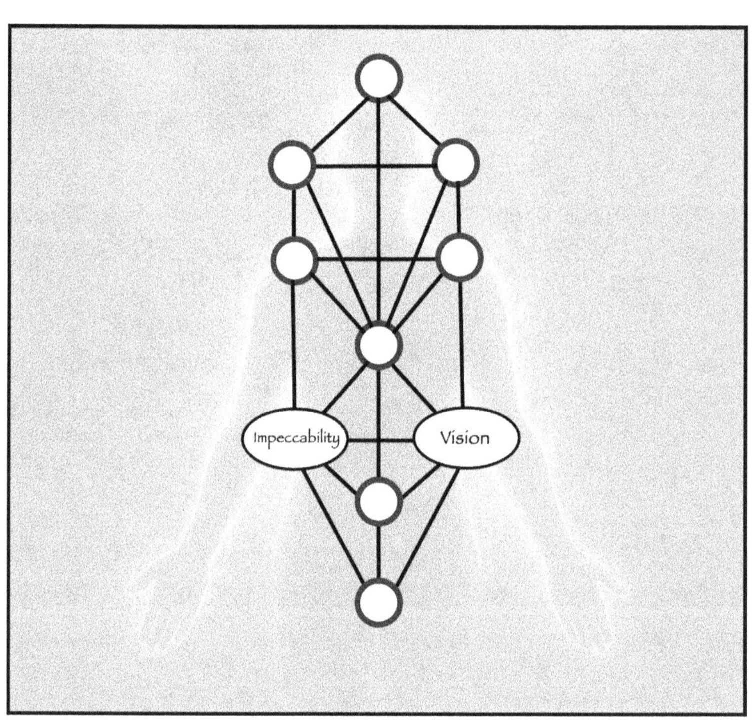

Impeccability
Vision

The Power of Impeccability and Vision: A Synergistic Approach

Our journey toward Excellence began with the question "**What** are our most important desires?" We then continued by asking, "**Why** do we want these desires to be fulfilled?", uncovering the deeper purpose behind these desires. Now, we arrive at the next step: "**How** can we bring these dreams into manifestation?"

This step invites us to harness the combined power of **Impeccability** and **Vision**— two essential elements for realizing our desires. Together they form the foundation of purposeful action, ensuring that our efforts are both precise and inspired.

"Impeccability: The Alchemy of Self-Mastery"

Long before I found myself teaching or mentoring others, back when I was just beginning to explore the deeper dimensions of human potential, I met someone who would forever shape my understanding of impeccability.

It was 1972, and I had heard whispers about a remarkable entity being channeled through a young man in Marin County. Out of curiosity, I decided to attend. What I found stunned me. Honesty, clarity, courage, humor and wisdom radiated from him like sunlight breaking through a fog.

It was his impeccability that drew me back, Sunday after

Sunday, for the next two years. Each week, I joined a small circle of seekers who, like me, were captivated by his authenticity. He spoke with a fearless conviction that I had never encountered before, wielding truth as both a scalpel and a balm. He challenged us, scolded us, inspired us, and loved us—all with a rawness that cut through our layers of pretense and conditioning.

Through him, I saw what it meant to embody human potential. He didn't just teach impeccability; he lived it. His humor was sharp and irreverent, his challenges relentless, his insights profound. He showed us—again and again—that it was possible to live from a place of absolute truth, unshackled by the ingrained behaviors that kept us from experiencing our authentic selves.

And just as unwavering as his teaching was his commitment to his promise. From the very beginning, he told us he had one mission: to awaken 100 people to their own potential.

He kept his word. Two years after we met, he announced that his work with us was done.

"You are ready now," he told us, his voice steady and resolute. "The ball is in your court."

We were devastated. We begged, pleaded, and cried, insisting that we weren't ready, that we still needed him. But nothing swayed him. True to his impeccability, he walked away, leaving us with a mixture of heartbreak and empowerment.

Even now, his impact remains undeniable. He occupies a special place in my heart, and my gratitude for him is as vibrant today as it was then. I often think of him and smile, wondering if we will meet again on the other side. Until then, I carry the lessons of his impeccability with me—a gift that continues to shape my journey.

Impeccability: Walking in Alignment

Impeccability isn't for the faint of heart. It's a path that calls us to live in coherence —to align the way we think, speak, feel, and act. By taking full responsibility for the reality we create through our thoughts, feelings, words and actions, we own our power. This path challenges us to fully embrace our desires, summon the courage to follow our hearts, and ensure that our motivations are clear and true. Once desire and intention are aligned, integrity becomes essential to the journey of manifestation. Impeccability means choosing each step with care, and act compelled and guided by the vision of our desire's successful realization.

Impeccability isn't a word we hear much these days. It speaks to something that seems undervalued lately: the unwavering commitment to walk one's talk and to do what one says without justifications, excuses, self-serving lies, or compromises of any kind. It requires being present and fully committed to our intentions, with a sense of responsibility and solid self-respect. In essence, impeccability is about living with integrity—bringing our thoughts, words, feelings, and actions into perfect alignment. This way of living takes honesty, courage, and discipline. It's not the easy path, and few succeed at it. But those who do become like beacons of light in the darkness, showing by example that it is possible to live a life of integration and power.

We can draw inspiration from modern heroes who embody impeccability in both adversity and achievement. Take Nelson Mandela, for instance. During his imprisonment on Robben Island, his discipline and composure remained unshaken, serving as a powerful testament to his integrity. Even in the face of extreme injustice, Mandela maintained his dignity and unwavering commitment to impeccable conduct, proving that true power lies in how we choose to respond to life's challenges.

Similarly, Serena Williams, one of the greatest tennis players in history, demonstrates impeccability through her relentless discipline and work ethic. Her focus extends beyond winning; she strives to embody excellence in how she conducts herself both on and off the court, setting an example of grace, determination, and integrity.

We also see impeccability in those who dedicate themselves to mastery. Consider the daily commitment of athletes, acrobats, musicians, and dancers, who train for countless hours to achieve excellence in their fields. Or the Shaolin masters, whose extraordinary control over their bodies seems to transcend normal physical limitations, reflecting years of unwavering practice and discipline.

Even in ancient times, impeccability was revered. Samurai warriors, guided by the strict code of *Bushido*, lived by virtues like honor, discipline, and integrity. For the samurai, impeccability meant that every action, no matter how small, was performed with full awareness and intention—turning the mundane into a reflection of their higher principles.

Impeccability is the commitment to act in alignment with our desires and the clarity of our intentions. It's about achieving coherence between our mind, emotions, and actions. When these aspects are fully aligned, they create a powerful harmony—a unity that drives both our purpose and our ability to manifest desires with integrity. Impeccability is not merely about what we do but about **HOW** we do it—infusing every action with dignity, presence, and power.

This principle comes to life in the story of a humble monk whose daily practice exemplified the essence of impeccable action.

"Sweeping the Temple Floor: A Lesson in Impeccability"

In a secluded mountain monastery, a monk began each morning by sweeping the temple floor. His movements were deliberate, each sweep of the broom an act of devotion.

One morning, after hours of careful work, a sudden gust of wind swept leaves and dust back across the floor he had just cleaned. A visiting traveler, observing the scene, exclaimed, "Oh, how terrible! You must be angry! All your hard work is undone!"

The monk looked up with a serene smile. "Undone? No, my friend. The purpose is not to finish the task but to do it impeccably."

And with that, he resumed sweeping, his movements calm and intentional, embodying the truth that impeccability is about the process, not the outcome.

Impeccability invites us to embody four essential disciplines—

pillars that align our inner and outer worlds as we walk the path of excellence.

- **Thought Impeccability:** Guarding our mind against negative and limiting thoughts. Instead, nurturing it with empowering, positive thoughts that align with our vision.
- **Word Impeccability:** Speaking with clarity, honesty, and kindness. Avoiding gossip, criticism, and negative self-talk. Letting our words support our desires, inspiring us to reach our goals rather than creating barriers.
- **Emotional Impeccability:** Fully embracing our emotions without judgment. Processing them with compassion, empowering those that are useful, and releasing those that no longer serve us.
- **Action Impeccability:** Taking consistent, inspired, and tangible steps towards our goals. Aligning our choices with our values, ensuring that our actions contribute to our well-being as well as to the greater good.

Vision: The Feminine Power of Attraction

It may start as a timid idea, slowly and gradually taking shape, or it may come as a surprising, full-blown vision. Yet nothing can ever be achieved without the power of attraction embodied by this feminine quality: vision.

What would impeccability be without a vision to inspire it and pull it forward through obstacles and challenges? It is only because of vision that we find the strength to persevere, to overcome difficulties, and to keep striving toward our goals.

Vision is what first lights the spark of desire within us. It is vision that helps us clarify our intentions, and it is vision that compels us to work with constancy and impeccability to manifest our dreams.

Vision is the lure, the magic, the magnet that makes everything seem possible. It sets into motion the energies of desire, clear intention, and active pursuit, presenting us with a glimpse of what could be. From her, all else flows.

This is why impeccability and vision are inseparable: without vision to guide and inspire it, impeccability would be lost and without purpose. Impeccability's masculine energy needs, wants, and yearns to serve its feminine muse—to act on her behalf, to strive to bring her vision to life. Through this sacred marriage of impeccability and vision, of masculine action and feminine creativity, we move toward excellence in a more balanced and harmonious way.

"A Vision of Beauty and Wonder"

Around the time of that powerful journey with the teacher who awakened my understanding of impeccability, a new kind of desire began to stir within me—one that would take shape not in a circle of seekers, but in the quiet, imaginative world of my young daughter.

She was four years old when I first felt the impulse that would lead me on an unexpected creative journey. Her room, with its plain walls and simple furniture, seemed to beg for something more—something magical, inspiring, and alive with imagination. I envisioned a space where her young mind could dream freely, where every corner would ignite her sense of wonder.

That vision fueled my steps. I began scouring the few second-hand shops in our small town, collecting old National Geographic magazines and any others I could find. I was searching for images that sparked something deep inside me—ones that felt alive with possibility. Piece by piece, I cut out these fragments of inspiration, collecting them into a growing treasure trove of ideas. I didn't know exactly what I was creating, but the desire to surprise and delight her, to gift her a space that could ignite her imagination, was my clear motivation.

As I began working, the process unfolded naturally, almost as if the images themselves were guiding me. My first collages were simple yet filled with love and intention. I crafted fantastical scenes that transported her walls into magical worlds—lush jungles, sparkling galaxies, whimsical landscapes where the impossible came alive. Seeing her eyes light up with joy at each new creation filled me with a sense of fulfillment I hadn't known before.

What began as a gift for her soon became something more. With every spare moment, I found myself cutting, arranging, and gluing. My creativity blossomed in ways I never anticipated, and my love for this art form grew fierce. It didn't matter where or on what I worked—scraps of cardboard, pieces of wood, even the back of an old notebook. Every surface became a canvas. My commitment was absolute, my efforts impeccable.

Over time, the process took on a life of its own. The collages seemed to make themselves, as though I were merely an instrument in the hands of some greater creative force. There was an effortless flow to the work, a grace and elegance that felt both thrilling and humbling. What had started as a personal project now felt like something much larger—a dance between inspiration and action, vision and manifestation.

Encouraged by friends, I took a courageous step forward. I began sharing my work in local art shows and competitions. It was daunting at first, to expose something so personal to the world, but the joy of sharing my creations far outweighed any fear. The feedback was overwhelmingly positive, and with each show, my confidence grew. This chapter of my life was alive with passion and fulfillment, a vibrant dance of beauty, wonder, and imagination.

For ten years, I poured myself into this art form. It became a defining part of who I was, and through it, I reached a level of excellence that transformed not just my work, but my sense of self. I saw myself as an artist, and for the first time, I truly believed it. The vision I had nurtured for so long had become my reality, and it brought me immense joy and empowerment.

But then, one day, the energy shifted. I sat down to create, and... nothing. The spark, the drive, the inspiration—it was simply gone. At first, I couldn't understand it. I waited for it to return, convinced it was just a passing phase. Days turned into weeks, then months, and still, the creative fire remained dormant. I felt a profound sense of loss, as though I had been abandoned by something I loved deeply.

Eventually, I had no choice but to let go. With time and reflection, I began to see that the space left behind wasn't empty. It was making room for something new. New opportunities, new visions, and new passions began to emerge, quietly at first, then with growing clarity. I realized that the chapter of collage-making, as beautiful as it was, had served its purpose. It had enriched my life, taught me about the power of vision, and prepared me for what was to come.

And so, I surrendered. I released the joy of making collages and stepped into the next chapter, trusting that life, in its infinite wisdom, was leading me where I needed to go. Looking back, I see it all with gratitude—those ten magical years of wonder and creation, and the lessons they carried. The vision had come full circle, leaving me richer for the journey.

Vision: The Illuminating Beacon

Having a vision is seeing the ultimate destination, envisioning a vivid picture of our personal or professional goal fully realized. It's the roadmap, the compass, guiding us through life's twists and turns.

A powerful vision is:

- **Clear:** Provides focus and direction.
- **Engaging:** Inspires and motivates.
- **Realistic:** Grounded in practical steps.
- **Inspiring:** Ignites hope and optimism.
- **Detailed:** Paints a vivid picture of the desired outcome.

A strong vision fuels our journey. It sustains us through challenges, invigorates us during triumphs, and illuminates our path, even in the darkest of times.

By incorporating impeccability and cultivating a powerful vision into our lives, we can unlock our full potential and embark on a journey of extraordinary achievement.

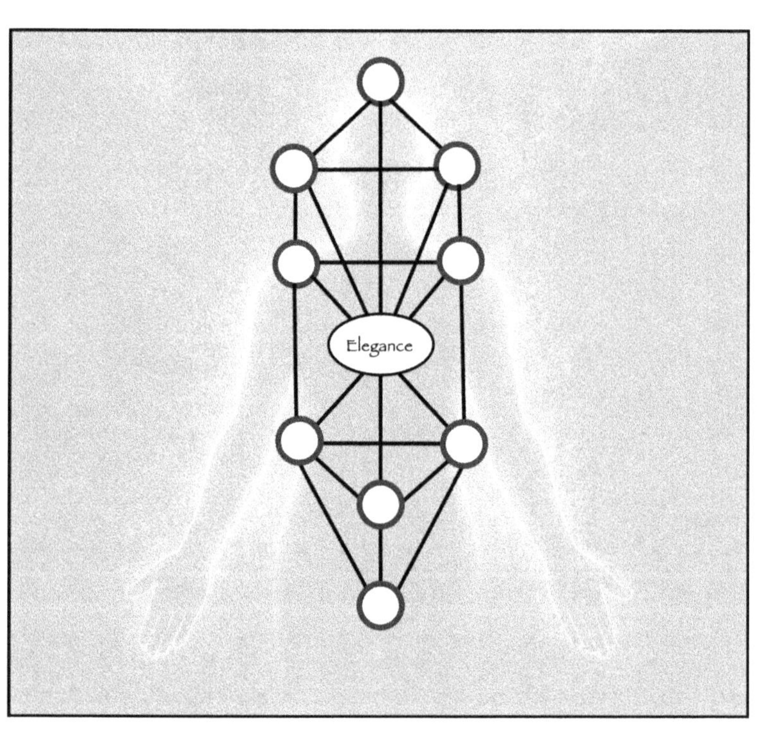

Elegance

4

Elegance: The Art of Manifesting with Grace

"Spontaneous fulfillment of Desire"

I had been living in Damanhur for nearly two years. A new rhythm had taken hold— one rooted in community, spiritual discovery, and creative expression. It was during this time that I woke up from a dream, my heart racing with the excitement of an extraordinary vision: to create a divination deck using the powerful symbols of the Damanhurian Sacred language.

The idea filled me with such joy and inspiration; it felt as though the universe itself had whispered it into my soul. Of all the deep knowledge and spiritual practices I encountered at Damanhur, one stood out for me: Sacred Language—a profound, ancestral ideogrammatic system that serves as a communication bridge to connect with Higher Forces in the universe.

The vision felt urgent and alive within me. As soon as I arrived at work that morning and saw Falco, the founder of Damanhur and a man of immense wisdom and creativity, I couldn't hold back. I shared my idea with him, explaining my desire to create this deck of cards that could serve as a tool for inner guidance. Since Falco had brought Sacred Language to Damanhur, it felt essential to ask his permission. To my delight, he was open to the idea and encouraged me to move forward.

Eager to bring the vision to life, I approached several of Damanhur's talented artists and asked them to create sample cards featuring Sacred Language symbols. While their efforts were beautiful, I noticed Falco wasn't particularly enthusiastic when I showed him the designs. Determined to find the right creative expression, I asked if I could use his selfic paintings as the background for the symbols. Falco's paintings were extraordinary—visionary works infused with energetic properties—and when he agreed, my excitement soared.

Buoyed by his support, I decided to share another dream that had been quietly growing in my heart. "Falco," I said, "I've always wanted to create a secondhand store here in Damanhur—a place to recycle clothes and items that people no longer need, giving them new life and making them available to the community." To my amazement, Falco immediately offered me a large, beautiful space that had previously been used for theater performances and community gatherings. I was speechless. With this encouragement, two of my deepest desires were set into motion.

The next year was a whirlwind of creativity and fulfillment. I transformed the given space into a thriving secondhand store, managing it with joy while simultaneously working on the oracle deck. Matching Falco's paintings with the perfect Sacred Language symbols became a meditative process, each card coming to life as if guided by unseen hands. I designed spreads, wrote a booklet explaining how to use the deck, and poured my heart into the project.

Falco was my steadfast supporter throughout, reminding me often, "I want the first deck so that I can 'prepare' it in the Temple." True to his word, when the project was completed a year later, I presented him with the very first printed deck. With a smile, he told me that he would place it in the Temple of Humankind, where it would be "prepared" energetically to be the anchor for all decks that would be sold, ensuring the cards would become the powerful and reliable tool they were meant to be.

The deck was a resounding success. With the support of two dear friends from Kauai, I had 3,000 decks printed. They've since become a cornerstone of my work, helping countless individuals access their inner wisdom and connect with their unconscious to find clarity and guidance.

Looking back, the entire project unfolded with a sense of effortless grace. Everything seemed to flow—each step falling into place with ease, each challenge met with unexpected support. It was as if the universe conspired to make my vision a reality. This experience taught me that when we align our desires with clear intention, act with commitment and impeccability, and trust the process, life responds with elegance. The journey wasn't just about manifesting a vision; it was about doing so with joy, wonder, and a sense of flow.

Elegance: The Graceful Path to Excellence

Elegance is rarely associated with personal or professional mastery, let alone spirituality. Too often, it's dismissed, overlooked, and judged as superficial—or worse, considered useless. Yet when we truly understand the value of elegance, we embrace the principle of least effort—where every action flows naturally and beautifully.

Elegance is about achieving our goals with grace and fluidity, aligning ourselves with the currents life presents to us. It is the balance between effort and ease, a harmonious dance that unfolds naturally. When elegance is present, our actions feel graceful and effortless.

They radiate self-confidence, self-respect, and most importantly, self-love.

Yet, my own journey to elegance was not without its challenges. For much of my life, I was addicted to struggle. My Catholic upbringing had conditioned me to believe that suffering pleased God, that poverty was a virtue, and that carrying one's cross in silence was the only way to earn divine favor while in this "valley of tears."

At the time, I didn't realize that we create our reality with our thoughts, beliefs, feelings, attitudes and actions. I moved through life embodying the victim-martyr role with great self-righteousness, convinced I was doing the "right" thing in God's eyes. I believed that my silent endurance of hardship would eventually be rewarded.

This commitment to struggle pervaded every area of my life: my finances, my relationships, my work, and—most of all—my mind and spirit. Joy was a stranger, happiness seemed impossible, and ease was a distant fantasy. I later realized that my attachment to struggle was directly tied to my inability to receive love. Despite the constant flow of life's gifts, I was blind to them, trapped in a narrative where struggle felt familiar and safe. Struggle was the daily nourishment for my inner victim and martyr, who embraced it as their natural state, convinced that this was the essence of life.

Thankfully, life has a way of waking us from unconscious slumber. Slowly but surely, I began to see the cracks in this unworkable pattern. A deep desire to break free from the self-imposed chains of distorted beliefs and attitudes arose within me. I became determined to love myself enough to allow life's blessings to flow into my existence.

I discovered that ease is a reflection of self-love. To embrace it, I had to feel the negative impact of my inability to receive love, confront the pain caused by that, and commit to healing it, nurturing my capacity for self-love. It took desire, clear intentions, commitment, and the vision of a lighter, more elegant life to embrace a reality free from stress and struggle.

The rewards were truly amazing! Once I opened myself to life's gifts, everything I wanted and needed began to flow to me with ease and grace. Miracles and synchronicities became part of my daily life—no longer rare events, but blessings I fully and gratefully accepted and received. I feel deeply blessed in every area of my life, which has continued to flow effortlessly since I awakened to this crucial element: **Elegance—the openness, willingness, and ability to embrace and receive the abundant love and blessings that life and the universe continually offer. In essence, *Elegance is self-love in action.***

Of course, you might say, "I've had plenty of successes in my life and achieved many of my desires." And I would respond, "Of course, I am sure you did. BUT were those successes achieved with **elegance**?" Only if the answer is yes can we say that you achieved them with **Excellence.**

Often, we desire with great intensity and feel clear about why we want what we want. We work hard to get results, striving diligently toward our goals. Our vision keeps us on track, reminding us not to give up. Yet, even with all these steps in place, we may find ourselves struggling, putting in relentless effort, blaming, complaining, competing, or resenting the challenges along the way. We might even achieve our goal and feel a sense of success, but the journey was without grace, without joy, and ultimately, without excellence.

One distorted belief we may be holding, and which is worth recognizing, is the idea that: "I do not deserve success unless I earn it, unless I work hard for it, **unless I deserve it**." But this isn't how the Universe works. The Universe is not busy deciding who deserves or doesn't deserve its gifts. Its abundance is available to anyone who is WILLING to receive it. It is this willingness to receive—not effort, struggle, or deserve-ability—that invites elegance into our lives and into the way we achieve our goals.

To walk the path of Excellence, Elegance is a crucial step. Its central place in the journey (and on the diagram) is no accident— it stands alone at the heart, as a vital element.

Without it, we cannot achieve our goals with true excellence.

Elegance is about loving ourselves enough to allow grace and ease to guide us to success. It requires the humility to recognize that we cannot achieve our goals alone. We need the support of life, the universe, and others. It is about opening our hearts to receive the love and guidance that is always available, helping us reach the finish line with greater ease and grace than we could ever achieve alone.

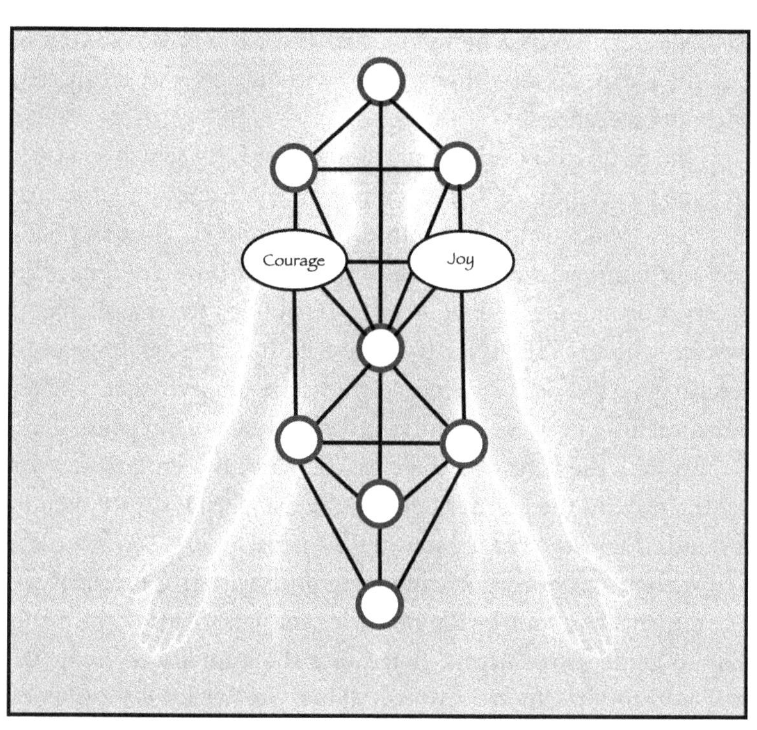

Courage
Joy

———————————————

5

The Dance of Courage
and Joy

———————————————

"Courage Unleashed. Joy Discovered."

Before my time in Kauai with Shakti Gawain—and even before the spontaneous fulfillment of my vision to create a divination deck using Damanhur's Sacred Language— there was a very different chapter of my life... a painful one.

It was when my 18-year marriage finally broke open...

It began with a confession that shook the very foundation of my world: my husband had fallen in love with a friend of ours.

This wasn't the first time that happened. Over the course of our 18-year marriage, there had been other flings—fleeting distractions that I had weathered with quiet patience, waiting for him to return, guilt-ridden and repentant. I had become accustomed to this rhythm, grudgingly accepting it as part of our life together.

But this time felt different. Familiar, yes, but with an intensity that unnerved me. His anguish was palpable as he wrestled with emotions he could neither contain nor reconcile. He didn't want to lose his family, yet he was drawn to her in a way he couldn't deny. For two agonizing months, we drifted in this unbearable limbo—neither moving forward nor finding resolution.

During those months, I retreated into my familiar role: the

"Victim/Martyr/Mother." I put on a brave face, masking the fear of abandonment clawing at my inner child. Beneath the facade of quiet understanding lay silent self-righteousness and judgement. This part of me was skilled at adapting—choosing to wait, watch and hope rather than act, risk, or take responsibility for what I truly wanted or needed. I delegated my power, letting him make the decisions, while convincing myself that patience was strength. But in truth, I was hiding— avoiding action and stifling my voice, unwilling to risk expressing my own feelings and needs. Beneath the surface, I buried the pain, disillusionment, and rising tides of anger, hoping that everything would somehow return to normal.

And then it happened… on a long drive to a friend's wedding, something in me finally snapped.

The tension in the car was suffocating, an invisible wall dividing us. Another conversation began, the same circular attempt to untangle the knots of our situation. His indecision was like quicksand, pulling us both down. Suddenly, as he spoke, something in me broke open. I couldn't do it anymore. I had reached the end of my rope. With nothing left to lose, I took a deep breath and let courage rise to the surface.

At first, it was the "Victim/Martyr/Mother" speaking— steady, restrained, and measured. I told him everything—the months of silent suffering, the hope I had clung to, the unbearable weight of waiting for him to choose. But, as the words poured out, something inside me broke free. The Silent and Repressed Straight Talker—the part of me that had long been muted—took over and stepped forward. The dam burst, and a tidal wave of raw emotion surged forth, unfiltered and unstoppable.

Years—decades—of suppressed anger and frustration erupted like a volcano, raw and uncontainable. It wasn't just about him or this moment; it was every betrayal, every disappointment, every time I had swallowed my feelings and put someone else's needs ahead of my own. My words were sharp, unrelenting, cutting through all the pretense and silence that I had chosen to allow in our marriage.

I have never before, nor ever again, unleashed such a volcano of fury as I did in that moment. I could hardly comprehend the floodgate of intensity that burst forth onto my soon-to-be ex-husband. It was a force I had never touched before—pure, undiluted rage, sharp, powerful, and as precise as a blade. It was uncontainable, unrestrained, unstoppable.

And then, in the very heart of that fiery explosion, something extraordinary happened.

Amid the storm of rage, time suddenly stopped. A deep stillness settled over me, and in an instant, I was flooded with something entirely unexpected—an overwhelming sense of peace and love. Not just any love, but unconditional, infinite, all-encompassing love.

I was love. I felt love, radiated love, became love. My mind, heart, and body were wrapped in exquisite bliss, an expansion of consciousness so vast and beautiful that words cannot contain it. It was nirvana, samadhi, enlightenment—whatever name you wish to give it. Love was the only reality.

My husband, of course, couldn't understand this sudden transformation. He thought it was a ploy, another strategy to manipulate the situation. He didn't believe for a moment that what I was exuding, saying, feeling, being, was real. But it was. Something fundamental within me had shifted. I went to the wedding in this remarkable state of bliss, carrying a joy so profound it felt otherworldly.

For three days, I lived an extraordinary state of grace. The courage to finally express my emotions—raw, unfiltered, and true—had unlocked a door I didn't even know existed. In its wake, all boundaries dissolved, leaving me enveloped in the profound Joy of oneness with 'All That Is' for those blessed, unforgettable days.

The Power of Courage, The Gift of Joy

On our journey toward the fulfillment of our desires with excellence, courage must be our steadfast companion. It empowers us to face fears, limitations, and difficulties with the understanding that the path may take time and involve overcoming significant challenges and uncertainties. With bravery and resilience, courage transforms obstacles into stepping stones on the road to mastery.

Progressing toward excellence requires more than the courage to confront challenges, discern, discriminate, and choose; it also demands the capacity to feel the joy of life itself— the joy of growth and the joy found in small victories along the way.

Courage embodies the masculine energy that enables us to overcome fear and obstacles, while joy reflects the feminine energy that makes the process enjoyable and fulfilling. Together, they form a dynamic partnership, sustaining our motivation and resilience.

While courage is a familiar concept, joy often remains elusive and misunderstood. We are more accustomed to pursuing happiness, which feels practical and justifiable, while joy is often dismissed as frivolous, even childish. Happiness is rooted in the satisfaction of our desires—an external achievement or experience that brings a sense of pleasure or relief. It's tied to outcomes: reaching a goal, acquiring something we longed for, or having our needs met.

Joy, however, arises from a deeper, more personal place. It's not about achieving or acquiring; it's about being. Joy flows from the fulfillment of our preferences—the things that uniquely resonate with who we are at our core. Unlike happiness, which depends on external circumstances, joy is an intrinsic experience that can exist even in the face of challenges or adversity.

This distinction is profound: happiness meets our basic survival needs and gratifies the external, while joy honors our inner world—our preferences, passions, and sense of purpose. Yet, because these preferences often feel impractical or indulgent, we dismiss them, burying our own source of joy beneath layers of self-judgment.

But here's the truth: it takes great courage to "follow our bliss." To prioritize joy is to honor what makes us feel truly alive, even when the world tells us it's not practical. And the reward for such bravery? A connection to something profound and unshakable—pure, unfiltered joy that transcends fleeting happiness and reminds us of the beauty and wonder of being fully ourselves.

When I reflect on moments when I had the courage to honor my preferences, I see that those were the times when joy was my reward. One such example is unfolding right now, as I write these very words.

"A Retreat into Joy"

Many years have passed since that fiery turning point in my marriage. Life has changed, softened, deepened. Now, after 24 years of living in Damanhur, I find myself nestled in the heart of Abano Terme, a charming little town in Italy, staying in a most wonderful hotel. For five glorious days, I've indulged in thermal baths, mud wraps, ozone therapy, and rejuvenating visits to steam and salt rooms, all capped off with massages by the hands of true professionals. The experience has been nothing short of heavenly.

But what does this have to do with courage and joy? It all began with a simple idea that flickered to life a couple of months ago: the possibility of spending time at a thermal resort. That thought sparked a strong desire—a preference I felt deeply compelled to pursue. With clear intention, I began searching for a place that was not only luxurious but also within my budget.

Courage played its part early. I approached my doctor with a bold question: might these treatments qualify for insurance coverage? To my delight, she agreed, offering a prescription that opened the door to possibility. Encouraged, I remembered an old friend who worked as a masseur in the region. Though we hadn't spoken in years, I reached out. To my amazement, not only was he still practicing, but he was employed at a prestigious hotel that he recommended I consider—especially during the more affordable low season.

It all came together seamlessly, almost as though the universe had been waiting for my courage to take the first step. I booked five days just before the Christmas holidays, and these few days have been nothing short of magical. From the exceptional daily treatments to three deeply healing massages with my friend, every moment has been a gift.

I've savored the thermal wellness areas, taken time for solitude and reflection, and even made space to write this book. Gratitude fills my heart, and a smile has rarely left my face. This isn't fleeting happiness—it's true joy. A joy that arose because I dared to trust my preferences, act on my desires, and let life meet me halfway.

"A Summer of Joyful Discovery"

This blissful spa retreat reminds me of another moment of joy—a few years earlier—born from the courage to prioritize a heartfelt desire. It began with a longing to visit my daughter in the United States—a dream I had nurtured for two years, since our last visit. This wasn't a casual wish but a deep preference, a clear intention to spend precious time together.

In my mind, I began shaping the vision: two months on the road with my daughter, exploring the beauty of national parks, camping under the stars, and reconnecting with old friends. The thought filled me with excitement and anticipation.

One day, as I shared this desire with my dear friend Ursula, she surprised me with an extraordinary offer: "I'll gift you a round-trip ticket to the U.S. in business class." I was stunned. Her generosity was overwhelming, and my old beliefs—those voices of unworthiness—immediately rose to protest.

"It's too much," they whispered. "How can you accept such a gift?"

Luckily, courage stepped in and soothed my doubts and concerns. It might seem strange that accepting such a generous gift required courage, but for me, it did. Years of conditioning and distorted beliefs in my own unworthiness whispered that it was too much, that I couldn't possibly say yes. Yet, it was precisely in facing those inner voices that courage became my ally, allowing me to accept the gift with gratitude and an open heart.

That summer became the stuff memories are made of. My daughter and I spent two unforgettable months traveling through nine states, visiting cherished friends, and marveling at the stunning landscapes of national parks. Whether we were pitching our tent under a canopy of stars or sharing quiet moments on a winding trail, joy was our constant companion.

Those months were a testament to the power of trusting and supporting my preferences. The courage to say yes, to honor my desires, and to let joy take the wheel, created memories I will treasure for a lifetime.

Most of the stories I've shared in previous chapters also involve courage—and whenever courage was present, joy was never far behind.

Take, for instance, the time in my early twenties when I left Italy for the United States with just a few bucks in my pocket. I was walking away from the most secure, rewarding, and cushioned job a young woman could have in Bologna. Yet, my desire to leave Italy, to venture into the unknown, became impossible to ignore. Everyone around me tried to dissuade me from what they saw as a reckless, impulsive decision—letting go of such a "lucky" situation for a leap into uncertainty. But I was adamant. I could no longer deny the call to something greater.

For me, the values of creativity and freedom outweighed the illusion of security that everyone else held so dear. Courage and naiveté walked hand in hand as I set out on this adventure—a decision that brought immense joy and a life I have never regretted choosing.

Another act of courage came years later, when I decided to leave my husband. I began packing my bags with no clear plan except a firm resolve: if it came to it, I would take a cab to a women's shelter. After months of waiting, compromising, and hoping things might change, I knew in my heart that the time had come. I had to leave. And then, as if the universe had been waiting for my decision, synchronicity stepped in. A phone call arrived at the perfect moment, changing the trajectory of my life forever. That leap of courage led to a future more joyful and rewarding than I could have imagined.

Courage was also my companion when the desire to return to

Italy overwhelmed me —this time to share the wonders of Voice Dialogue with my people. The pull was so strong that nothing could hold me back—not the love of my dear friend Shakti, not the sorrow of leaving the beautiful island of Kauai, nor my vow never to return to live in Italy. Even the lack of financial resources, the uncertainty of whether I would find interest or acceptance, or the heartbreak of leaving so much behind didn't deter me. Courage gave me the strength to face those fears and take the leap. And the years that followed, sharing Voice Dialogue in Italy, brought joy so profound and fulfilling that it nourished my soul in ways I could never have anticipated.

Then came the time to start over—at 56. When I arrived at Damanhur, I realized nothing I had done before held relevance in this new chapter. It was a complete stripping away of my old identity. I had to begin anew, like a newborn, learning a new language, adapting to a communal lifestyle, embracing a new spiritual vision, and immersing myself in courses to align with this unfamiliar reality. Joy came later—when all that learning bore fruit, allowing me to bring Damanhur's courses and message to the world.

And it didn't stop there. Returning to the United States years later with a new message and a fresh approach to life also required courage. Sharing teachings from an unfamiliar perspective, traveling the world with a mission to inspire growth and healing for humanity and the planet—this was no small undertaking. Courage carried me through, and the joy of witnessing transformation in others made it all worthwhile.

Every one of these leaps required courage—a willingness to face fear, risk being uncomfortable, and embrace the unknown. And in every case, joy followed as the reward: joy in the freedom to live authentically, joy in fulfilling a deeper purpose, and joy in knowing I had honored the call of my soul.

Think for a moment about the joy you feel when witnessing someone achieve a hard-earned goal. Picture the radiant expressions, the body language, the triumph in their eyes. Whether it's winning a game, passing a difficult test, or overcoming a significant challenge, their joy is palpable. Can you feel your own heart swell as you witness their triumph, as if their joy radiates outward and touches something deep within you? It's as though their courage becomes a shared experience, and their joy invites you to celebrate alongside them.

Courage and joy walk hand in hand on the path to excellence. Yet, while we often embrace courage, many of us have more difficulty allowing joy into our lives. Sometimes, we even fear it—afraid that the ecstatic high of joy might be followed by a deep sense of loss or even depression. It's as if we guard our hearts against joy, thinking it too fleeting, too risky. But the truth is, it takes courage to fully experience joy.

We can, however, infuse our journey toward excellence with joy by celebrating each moment of progress. Joy doesn't have to wait for the destination—it can be the sustaining force that nurtures our spirit, carrying us forward every step of the way. By choosing to find joy in every step, no matter how small, we enliven our quest for excellence. Each milestone, no matter how minor, becomes a reason to celebrate—a moment to pause, breathe, and smile.

Prioritizing our preferences with courage ensures a joyful and sustainable journey. When we embrace the process, finding delight in our progress and honoring each step forward, we create a positive, uplifting momentum that carries us closer to realizing our desires. Joy isn't just the reward for excellence; it's the fuel that propels us there.

As we reflect on Courage and Joy, it becomes clear that these two forces are not separate, but deeply connected, each enriching the other. Together, they guide us through life's uncertainties and illuminate the path toward our highest potential. In honoring both, we find liberation—not just from fear, but into the boundless possibilities of our authentic selves.

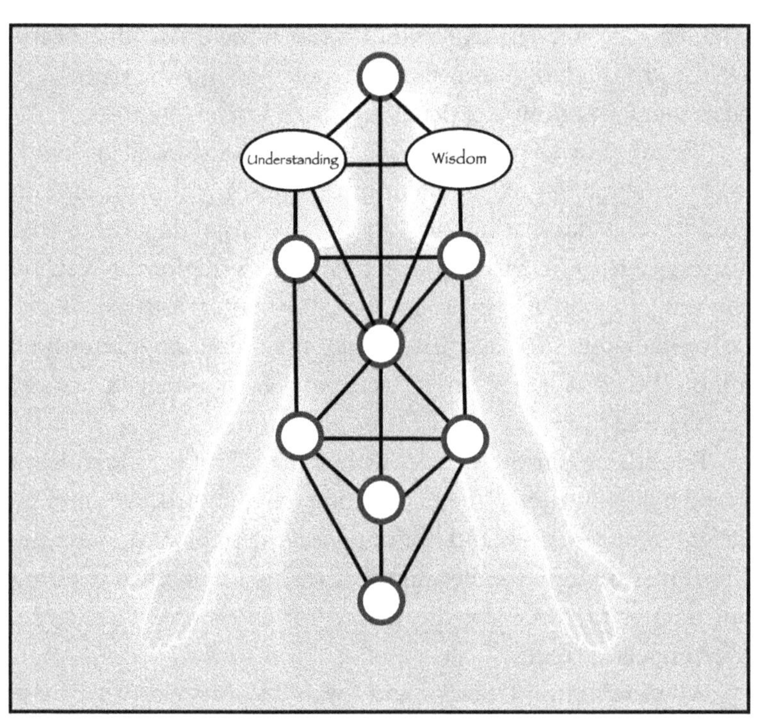

Understanding
Wisdom

6

The Alchemy of Understanding and Wisdom

Cultivating Understanding, Living Wisdom

The journey towards excellence is not merely a cognitive exercise but a deeply meaningful and emotional experience. It unfolds step by step: you have defined your desire, clarified your motivation for pursuing it, chosen a strategy or method to achieve it, focused on your vision with elegance, strengthened your courage, and embraced the joy of the journey. Now, the time has come to step into the realms of Understanding and Wisdom.

As we delve deeper into these realms, we unlock the profound potential of our true being, discovering the deeper truths that guide and inspire our path.

Understanding invites us to think, comprehend, and mentally elaborate on the entire process. This step is essential because the mind, when satisfied and at ease, becomes wiling to trust wisdom. Only then can wisdom operate in harmony with the mind; guiding, grounding, and solidifying what we have learned or understood.

Understanding serves as a bridge between the conscious and the subconscious mind. It illuminates the dark corners of our psyche, revealing the hidden patterns and beliefs that shape our reality. When we truly understand ourselves, we awaken the power to transform our lives.

Wisdom, by contrast, is the distilled essence of our experiences. It's the quiet voice of intuition, the gentle guide that helps us navigate life's labyrinth. Wisdom goes beyond knowledge—it is the compassionate application of knowledge, tempered with discernment and rooted in a deeper awareness.

Understanding and Wisdom are not abstract ideals—they are living principles that come alive through our experiences. This became profoundly clear to me during a pivotal moment in my life.

"A Deeper Dive into Understanding and Wisdom"

Few will ever forget where they were when the world came to a standstill. It was March 2020 when COVID became a global reality, sweeping across borders and lives, changing everything. I had just returned home from what I didn't realize at the time would be my final trip teaching Damanhurian courses—something I'd cherished doing for the past 15 years. As lockdowns took hold and we were all confined to our homes, the realization settled in: a chapter of my work had ended, fading away naturally, quietly, like a gentle exhale.

At first, the stillness felt unfamiliar. Without trips to plan or destinations to reach, my days stretched out before me, unstructured and open. But in that space of quiet, something began to stir. A forgotten part of me, like an old melody resurfacing, started to hum again.

Slowly, a desire emerged—to revisit the teachings that had shaped my life so profoundly since the early 1980s.

This rekindling felt electric, as though a dormant ember of my soul had been reignited. The longing to share these transformative teachings filled me with purpose. It was as if a part of me, long asleep, had been gently nudged awake, eager to contribute to the collective journey of evolution.

Back then, Lazaris had been my guide—a teacher whose

wisdom and humor lit up my world. For eight years, I immersed myself in his teachings, captivated by the clarity he brought even to the most intricate metaphysical truths. Lazaris had a way of breaking down complex ideas into practical, actionable steps, guiding us through the **understanding** necessary to integrate these truths into our lives.

As I pulled out my old notebooks, their pages worn and marked with the scribbles of a younger me, I felt as though they were alive—whispering to me, inviting me to share their gifts once again. A deep connection to the wisdom within the material stirred something profound in me. The teachings seemed to leap off the page, vibrant and full of life, as if they'd been waiting for this very moment.

With great excitement, I began effortlessly crafting new courses from those notes, weaving in exercises and meditations to bring the teachings to life. It felt as though a deeper, more grounded understanding of those principles was unfolding within me, providing a solid foundation and renewed confidence to embark on this next chapter of my journey.

The first course I created, *From Self-Awareness to Self-Realization*, was a labor of love. It brought together my favorite teachings of Lazaris, and with the invaluable help of my dear friend Shoco, I transformed it into an online course. At a time when in-person gatherings had ceased and the world had shifted to virtual spaces, the timing couldn't have been better. The course resonated deeply with participants and was a success.

Encouraged by this response, I eagerly began adapting more of Lazaris's material. This led to the creation of *Conscious Co-Creation*, a course designed to empower people to consciously shape their reality. I had found my niche! I was taking teachings that had profoundly shaped my own life and, with a fresh understanding, transforming them into courses that inspired me and ignited my passion for sharing these transformative tools with others.

The more I worked with these teachings, the deeper my connection to them grew. I came to understand their depth and value on a much more conscious level, not just as concepts I had studied but as truths I was now living. Although I had worked with this material since I first encountered it, it now felt like a powerful and transformative reality—a solid foundation guiding both my life and my work.

My deeper understanding of these teachings brought a clarity that made living them both effortless and deeply rewarding. Their wisdom became a steady guide, leading me toward greater ease and freedom in my daily life. They were no longer just theories or abstract concepts—they had become a way of life, a reality that completely filled me with purpose and joy.

I felt immense gratitude to Lazaris for sharing these teachings with me at a time when I needed them most. They had been seeds of transformation, guiding me through years of growth and discovery. Now, so many years later, I wasn't just studying or applying them—I was truly living them and sharing their gifts with others. This integration allowed their wisdom to shine as a natural, guiding light in my life, illuminating not only my own path but the paths of those I had the honor to teach.

The Mind's Journey to Stillness and Wisdom

The mind is a remarkable tool and an essential element in the journey toward excellence. After all, every creation begins with an idea—a thought that holds immense potential for realization. The mind's role is to explore the possible choices before us, considering their impact, the strategies available, and the potential consequences. At its core, the mind seeks security, working to create a sense of stability and ease. Understanding comes from gathering knowledge, insights, and information that help us feel more confident and capable of managing our reality.

When the mind feels it has understood, it can relax, letting go of its need for control. In this openness, wisdom naturally begins to emerge, adding a deeper clarity, meaning, and purpose to what we have come to understand.

Wisdom is not something handed to us by others or learned

solely from books. It arises from within, a deeper perception rooted in our innate intelligence always available to guide us. This quiet knowing is something we can trust and rely upon, a steady presence that illuminates our path with clarity and grace.

"A Moment of Grace: The Gift of a New Name"

Many years ago—long before coming to Damanhur, online courses or global lockdowns—I was drawn to Montana for a two-week Summer Camp led by my dear friend Brooke Medicine Eagle. It was a gathering of simplicity and connection—a small group singing heartfelt songs, learning native crafts, and deepening our relationship with the elements of earth, fire, air, and water. The experience was a nurturing balm for body, mind, and soul, a return to the roots of being.

One evening, under the luminous glow of a Full Moon, we made a collective decision: we would spend the entire night outdoors, bundled in our sleeping bags around the campfire. Each of us took turns tending the fire for an hour, ensuring its warmth and spirit were kept alive through the night.

When it was my turn—midnight to 1 a.m.—I was gently woken by the person before me. Groggy but eager, I wrapped myself in a shawl, went to the drum, and settled by the fire. The rhythm of the earth's heartbeat seemed to flow naturally from my hands as I began to drum softly, the steady sound resonating through the stillness of the night.

As I watched the flickering flames, something shifted within me. The drum's beat began to carry me, and without effort, a soft chant emerged from my lips. The chant flowed effortlessly, shaping itself into a mantra that I found myself repeating again and again, as if the words were rising from some deep well of knowing. The mantra fit perfectly with the drum's rhythm, the two weaving together in a harmonious flow.

In that hour, I entered a gentle trance, fully present yet carried beyond the ordinary. The fire, the drum, and the mantra seemed to hold me in a sacred space. It was only as my time ended, when I rose to wake the next fire keeper, that I realized what I had been chanting. The words flowing from my lips were not random—they were my new name: TerraLuna (EarthMoon).

I was elated, filled with a profound sense of awe and gratitude. I realized I had been given a precious gift, one that could only emerge through the gentle guidance of my inner Wisdom. It was this deep, intuitive knowing that had opened my body, mind, and spirit, allowing me to receive such an extraordinary offering.

The energy coursing through me was electric, and sleep was impossible that night. My heart was alive with the rhythm of the drum, with my new name's magical revelation, an experience which had ignited a flame within me that could not be extinguished.

When I returned to my home in Hawaii, there was no hesitation. The very first thing I did was legally change my last name to Terraluna—a name filled with meaning and resonance, one that reflected the profound connection to the wisdom that flows through us when we are truly open. To this day, Terraluna remains a part of me, a living reminder of that transformative moment under the Full Moon's light.

That experience was a testament to the power of intuition and the transformative nature of wisdom. It was a reminder that when we open ourselves to the rhythms of the universe, we receive gifts beyond our wildest dreams.

Wisdom is a quiet, steady presence—an expansive sense of oneness and being-ness. It deepens our connection with spirit, whispering intuitive guidance from the larger vision of our soul. Wisdom is a knowing beyond the mind, surpassing the rational and the intellect. It fills the body, mind, and heart with a profound sense of rightness, peace, depth, and solidity.

It does not question; it simply knows.

Wisdom perceives beyond what our eyes can see, hears whispers our ears cannot grasp, and touches spaces within us that we rarely know how to access. It emerges from within, often surprising us with its clarity and insight, guiding us unerringly on the path to excellence.

By cultivating both understanding and wisdom, we gain the ability to navigate life's challenges with grace and resilience. We transform suffering into joy, fear into courage, and limitations into boundless possibilities. Together, understanding and wisdom illuminate the path to a life of profound purpose, alignment, and limitless potential.

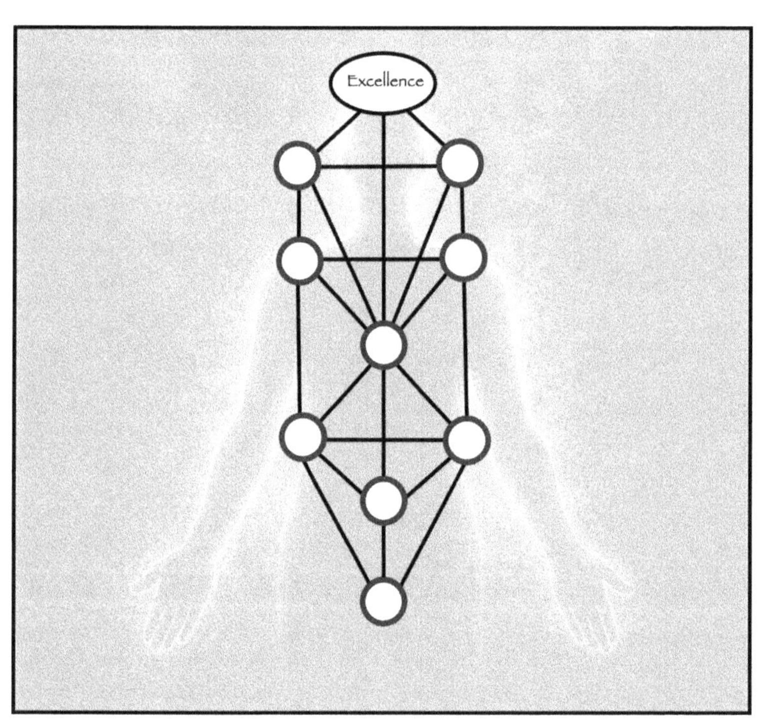

Excellence

7

Living Excellence: The Journey That Never Ends

Excellence is more than an achievement—it is a way of being, one that transcends ordinary limitations and moves beyond the constraints of the ego and conventional logic. It is the pure expression of our human potential, a force that compels us toward mastery. It begins with desire, is shaped by clear intention, and comes alive through impeccability and vision. It unfolds with elegance, is infused with courage and joy, and is deepened through understanding and wisdom. When we embody these qualities, we step fully into Excellence, allowing it to manifest effortlessly in our lives.

Excellence brings the profound satisfaction of personal growth and transformation. It is the pursuit of our highest aspirations and the embodiment of the very qualities that lead us there. When we walk this path, we honor our desire, move with clear intention, act with impeccability, trust our vision, live with elegance, express courage, feel joy, deepen our understanding, and share our wisdom naturally. Excellence is not a distant peak to conquer but the very path beneath our feet—it is the journey itself.

I didn't always understand Excellence in this way. But not too long ago, something within me stirred, drawing me back to a forgotten wisdom that had once ignited a spark in me...

"Rekindling Excellence"

One morning, as the golden light of dawn filtered through my window, I woke up with a deep, undeniable pull toward something I hadn't revisited in years—the Excellence Process. It had been decades since I first encountered it in the early 80s, during the monthly Lazaris gatherings I used to attend with such eagerness. At the time, though the process had left a strong impression on me, my focus had been elsewhere—on *The Valued Self,* a path of self-enhancement that many years later would become the foundation for my seven-week course, *From Self-Awareness to Self-Realization*.

Now, something within me stirred, urging me to return to those early teachings, to re-engage with the wisdom that had once ignited a spark in me. I felt a longing to reconnect, to delve deeper into the power of Excellence—not just as a concept, but as a way of being.

I went to my bookshelf and pulled out my old notebooks, their pages yellowed with time, carrying the echoes of past insights. Flipping through them, I searched eagerly for notes from the *Excellence Weekend*, hoping to find the teachings transcribed in my own hand. But as I turned page after page, my anticipation gave way to disappointment. There was nothing.

No detailed reflections, no written explanations—only a single, rough pencil sketch.

It was a diagram—one I had drawn long ago, depicting the *Excellence Process* superimposed on the *Tree of Life*. I stared at it for a long moment, feeling a twinge of regret that I hadn't recorded more. And yet, something about that simple sketch held a quiet power.

It wasn't just an image; it was a portal, a key to something profound that I had once understood and now longed to remember.

Determined to bring it back to life, I searched online for a clear pattern of the *Tree of Life* and printed a fresh copy. With care, I transferred each element of the *Excellence Process* onto the spheres of the *Tree of Life*, placing them as Lazaris had shown us all those years ago.

Then, I pinned the chart onto my vision board where I could see it every day.

Something shifted.

Each time I looked at it, a wave of recognition washed over me. The symbols spoke to me beyond words, stirring an understanding deeper than thought. I felt a resonance with the material —almost as if the teachings themselves were reaching out, inviting me to remember their full depth.

Then, one day, my friend Shoco came to visit. As we sat together, I found myself eagerly sharing my journey of rediscovery, recounting my process of reconnecting with these powerful principles. I showed her the pattern, tracing my fingers over the placements, and as I spoke, my enthusiasm grew. I could feel the energy of the material coming alive in my words.

Shoco listened intently, her eyes lighting up with the same excitement that was coursing through me. Then, with her characteristic clarity and decisiveness, she said, *"Shama, this is powerful. If you put together a course on this, I'll help you promote it."*

Her proposal landed like a spark igniting dry tinder. The moment she said it, I knew it was right. It was as if all the pieces had been waiting for this exact moment to fall into place.

I agreed instantly.

With a renewed sense of purpose, I began writing the course. The process was effortless, exhilarating. Each day, as I worked, I felt the steps of Excellence unfolding in my own life. My *desire* to share this material was unwavering. My *intention* was crystal clear — to pass on a formula that could uplift and empower others. I worked with *commitment and impeccability*, refining the content until it resonated with precision. My *vision* of bringing this course into the world fueled my enthusiasm, and the work unfolded with *elegance and grace.*

Fear never entered the equation—only *courage and joy.* Each insight deepened my *understanding*, and as I continued, a profound *wisdom* emerged, guiding me through the process. I was not just teaching *Excellence*—I was *living it.*

In just one month, the course was complete.

With Shoco's invaluable support, we presented it to a group of eager participants, and the response was immediate—excitement, gratitude, recognition. I watched as the material took root in their lives, bringing power and clarity to their personal and professional journeys. It was not just they who were enriched—I was, too.

My personal journey that has led to the creation of this course has been decades in the making—each chapter of my life shaped by the very qualities explored in these pages. As I brought the course to life, it became clear that Excellence isn't just a concept I've studied— it's a path I've walked. And perhaps nothing has brought that home more clearly than a recent experience, one that felt like a radiant expression of living Excellence in action.

"A Truly Excellent Birthday Gift"

My birthday is just five days away, and I find myself overflowing with joy and gratitude. Life has been showering me with blessings, and I feel called to share one of them with you—a gift that, for me, embodies the living energy of Excellence.

About a month ago, I received a message from an old friend in the U.S., inviting me to represent Damanhur in a new organization she was helping to create. Its mission— spreading gender equality and peace across the globe—spoke to my heart. With the blessing of Damanhur's leadership, I accepted the invitation with a deep sense of honor. Soon after, I began attending their weekly meetings.

It was during the first of these gatherings that I met an indigenous woman who had visited Damanhur in the past. Our connection was immediate, full of warmth and recognition.

She invited me to an Indigenous Gathering in the Yucatán, scheduled for the Spring Equinox.

From the moment she mentioned it, something inside me

stirred—a clear and unmistakable "yes." The cost was high, but the calling was stronger. I followed my intuition and booked the ticket.

Around the same time, I learned that one of my most beloved teachers, Matías De Stefano, would also be in the region during the Equinox, hosting his own celebration. Though I had already committed to the Indigenous Gathering, part of me longed to be near Matías and the powerful energy of his work. But the logistics made it feel impossible—I would be without a car, fully engaged with the Elders, and in a different location altogether.

Still, I allowed myself to hold the vision quietly, trusting life to guide the way.

And then, it happened—life answered with one of those rare, breathtaking moments of alignment.

Scrolling through Matías' chat group, I saw an announcement that made my heart leap: he had invited the very same Elders I would be with to join him for his Equinox celebration on March 20th. I read it twice, hardly believing it was true. My dream, my desire, my whispered prayer... had come to life.

I was going to experience both. I didn't have to choose. Life had found a way to weave them together—more gracefully than I ever could have planned.

A wave of joy and gratitude washed over me. In that moment, I felt seen by the universe—deeply seen, supported, and celebrated. It wasn't just a personal victory. It felt like a confirmation that when we live in alignment with desire, clear intention, and trust, life meets us with grace.

And the gifts kept coming.

I was soon invited to a Zoom call with the Indigenous Grandmother and a kind man I had once sponsored during his visit to Damanhur. He had now arranged for me to stay with a gracious host in Cancún on my first night. As we spoke and deepened our connection, we discovered a surprising link: we all shared a teacher from my past—someone who continues to guide them today.

This journey, I've come to see, is more than personal. It is a bridge—connecting ancient Indigenous wisdom with the spiritual technologies and teachings of Damanhur. Matías has visited Damanhur twice and feels aligned with our mission. Now I find myself standing in the center of these worlds, humbly carrying energy and understanding between them. A messenger. A weaver. A bridge.

As I prepare to celebrate my birthday, I do so with a heart full of purpose, joy, and love—not only for the beauty of what's unfolding in my life, but for the deeper meaning behind it. This is what Excellence feels like in motion: not a pursuit of perfection, but a dance with synchronicity, trust, and grace.

It is clear to me that Excellence can be pursued in every area of life—whether in meditation or cooking, in creating art or engaging with others, in social activities, sports, dancing, or the work we do each day. It can be present in the way we raise children, care for the sick, and show up for life itself. But Excellence is not passive; it calls us to step beyond our comfort zones, to claim our power, gifts, talents, and dreams so that they may work through us, rather than remain untapped potential. It challenges us to reach higher, to seek more meaningful results, to confront limiting beliefs, to face our fears, and to choose with courage. Along the way, it transforms our habits, reshapes our thoughts, and refines our convictions, attitudes, and behaviors.

Yet, the journey to Excellence is not one of rigid discipline alone—it is one of discovery, joy, and passion. It invites us to stretch beyond mediocrity, to embrace growth with enthusiasm, and to step into a fuller version of ourselves. As we walk this path, Excellence has the power to elevate our self-esteem, deepen our self-love, strengthen our confidence, and enhance our self-respect. It brings meaning to our life, empowers our choices, expands our awareness, and leads us to a life far beyond what we once imagined possible.

In this moment—at this stage of my life—I see Excellence not as a destination but as a faithful companion, always calling me to rise.

I am deeply grateful to Lazaris for sharing his wisdom, sparking in me an enduring desire to explore each element of

Excellence at a profound level. That spark became a journey—one that allowed me to embody these teachings fully so that I could pass them on, not as theory, but as lived experience.

I hope that if this book has found its way into your hands, you are ready to explore Excellence as a path of personal growth and self-empowerment. If I have shared these concepts clearly enough for you to embrace—as a guide toward your own inner freedom— then I am truly fulfilled.

Part II
YOUR JOURNEY TOWARDS EXCELLENCE BEGINS...

Excellence isn't something you master overnight. It's a way of living, one conscious choice at a time.

~ Shama Viola

Note to the Reader

You've just traveled through my own story. Now, this book becomes your guide.

What follows is not a rigid path, but a living map for your personal unfolding. Each lesson offers a key—one of the Seven Steps of Excellence—to explore and embody in your everyday life. This is a journey of reflection, revelation, and realization. Let it unfold at your own pace.

You might move through one step per week or spend longer with the ones that call to you most deeply. You may wish to invite a friend or form a small circle to explore the steps together—sharing insights can amplify your growth. Most importantly, listen to your own inner rhythm. Let the process be alive and responsive to you.

As you engage with the prompts and practices, keep a dedicated notebook nearby. Let it become a companion on this path, a mirror for your inner discoveries. There is no "right" way—only your way.

This is not a race. It's an invitation to deepen. Welcome to your journey.

8

Lesson One

THE SPARK OF BECOMING - HONORING DESIRE

Desire is the first breath of transformation. It's the whisper that stirs you from slumber, the ember that hints at a fire waiting to be lit. Without desire, nothing begins.

We've often been taught to mistrust our desires—to see them as selfish, excessive, even dangerous. But what if desire is not a flaw, but an impulse asking to be trusted? What if it is the soul's compass, quietly pointing us toward the life that wants to unfold through us?

Desire is not idle wishing—it is the red flame at the base of your spine, the vital force that awakens will and fuels action. It gives direction and energy to your path. When embraced consciously, desire becomes the foundation of clarity, commitment, and growth.

This first step on the journey of Excellence invites you to enter into a more honest relationship with desire   not as fantasy or fleeting longing, but as a guiding current. Your desire may be bold or quiet, immediate or expansive. What matters is that it is real—alive within you.

Take your time with this step. The reflections and practices that follow are meant to help you discern the essence of what you truly want—not just the surface form, but the deeper yearning underneath. The clearer and more resonant your desire, the more it will sustain you on the path ahead.

Some questions may not apply or feel relevant to your process. Simply choose the ones that resonate with you, and feel free to skip the rest.

Keep your journal nearby. Choose one desire at a time to explore fully.

~

Reflect & Clarify: WHAT Do I Truly Desire?

- What do I truly desire, imagine, or expect at this particular moment in my life? (These can be tangible or intangible—list up to three, but choose one to focus on for this process.)
- Can I clearly define what I want?
- What is fueling this desire?
- Is this desire really mine, or is it shaped by others' expectations?
- Is it a genuine calling, or more of a wish or idea?
- What do I imagine will happen once I fulfill this desire?

Explore the Shadows: What Stands in the Way?

Sometimes, even as I long for something, part of me resists receiving it.

- What part of me might not want this, deep down?
- What fears, doubts, or inner conflicts are stirred by this desire?
- What has kept me from creating or allowing this until now?

- What beliefs, habits, or patterns might be standing in the way?
- What do I gain from not having this? (*For example: avoiding responsibility, staying in familiar territory, protecting myself from judgment or envy, holding onto an identity that feels safe—even if it's limiting.*)

What Do I Believe About This Desire?

My beliefs shape how I approach desire—either fueling it or holding it back.

- What do I believe about the possibility of this desire becoming real?
- What thoughts do I hold about my ability to achieve it?
- What do I believe about whether I deserve to receive this?
- What convictions do I carry about what it takes to fulfill this desire? (*For example: "I have to work hard," "It will require struggle," or "It must come easily to be meant for me."*)

Emotional Check-In: What Do I Feel?

- Do I feel excited, joyful, or energized when I think of this desire?
- Or do I feel hesitant, overwhelmed, or afraid?
- Am I more afraid of failing—or of actually succeeding?
- What excites me most about this desire?
- How easily do I allow myself to feel excitement —and trust it as valid guidance?

What Is My Attitude or Approach Toward the Path Ahead?

Desire invites movement—but how I approach the path matters just as much as the destination.

- What is my attitude toward the tests, challenges, or risks that may arise?
- What approach am I bringing—bold and committed, or hesitant and uncertain?
- What patterns have shaped my journey so far in regard to desire in general and this desire in particular? *Do I tend to begin with enthusiasm but stop halfway? Do I adapt, postpone, or hold back when momentum builds?*
- What gets triggered when I imagine walking this path all the way through? *Does it stir fear, excitement, resistance, a sense of responsibility—or something else entirely?*

Readiness & Willingness: Am I Prepared to Begin?

Desire is only potential until I choose to act. This reflection helps me sense my readiness.

- What signs show me I'm ready to move toward this—despite discomfort or challenge?
- What am I willing to change, release, or grow into in order to allow this into my life?
- What level of commitment feels true right now—what am I genuinely prepared to give?

Aligned Action: What Will I Do?

This is where desire meets the ground—where vision begins to take shape through action.

- What energy, time, or attention am I willing to offer this desire?
- What structures, habits, or comforts might I need to release or revise?
- What actions feel aligned with this desire—and what actions do not?
- What is one practical, meaningful step I can take now?
- What would help me begin—today, this week, or in the near future?

Essence of the Desire: What Am I Really Seeking?

Beneath every desire lives a deeper yearning—a soul-level quality we long to experience or embody.

- What is the essential quality this desire holds for me? *(Joy? Belonging? Peace? Security? Freedom?Creativity? Power? Love?)*
- What do I imagine this desire will bring me—not just in form, but as an experience?
- Is that quality already present somewhere in my life, even in a small way?
- Can I name the true essence of what I'm longing for beneath the surface?

Creative Integration Exercise: Build Your Vision

- Create a vision board for each desire you have found. (Focus on one desire at a time)
- Choose images that inspire you, energize you, and awaken the feeling of your desire.
- You can add words that hold meaning and offer encouragement on your path.
- You might also draw, paint, or include any symbols that help bring your vision to life.
- Let this be a creative, intuitive process—a reflection of your inner longing made visible.

Enjoy this process and have fun with it!

Optional Explorations: If Your Desire Feels Unclear

1. The Imagination Game
   - Write a short story where anything is possible. Let your imagination run wild. Don't censor it. Trust what emerges—even if it's silly, bold, or unexpected.
2. The Desire Inventory
   - Make a list of every desire you have right now—big or small. Include everything that comes to mind, even things that may seem mundane, impractical, or fleeting. Nothing is too trivial or too bold. Just let the desires pour onto the page without judgment. This is simply a way to begin listening more deeply to what is alive in you right now.
   - Look over your list of desires and mark each one with one of the following letters:
     - **F** — for those that have been **fantasies:**

desires you've held for a long time but haven't taken any real action toward.

- **S** — for those you **seldom act upon**: they arise from time to time, but you rarely give them your energy or attention.
- **D** — for the desires that feel like **true desires**: ones you genuinely want to act on and bring into reality.
  - Choose one true desire ("D") and take a small step to honor it.

3. Creative Vision Board
   - Even if you are unsure of what you want, you can follow what draws you. Let colors, images, and textures speak for what words you may not yet know. Trust the creative process.

Closing Reflection: The Invitation of Desire

Desire begins with a whisper—sometimes clear, sometimes barely audible. But even the faintest longing carries the seeds of change.

To name what you want is to begin listening more deeply to yourself. To follow that thread is to allow life to move through you in a new way.

This is not about grasping or striving. It's about awakening a felt sense of what is ready to emerge. Honoring desire is not the end goal—it is the beginning of alignment, the first stirring of a path forming beneath your feet.

Let desire be your invitation. Walk with it. Listen to it. Let it lead you—gently, truly, into the next unfolding of who you are.

9

Lesson Two
CLEAR INTENTION - REFINING THE COMPASS OF MOTIVATION

If desire is the spark, intention is the compass—it gives direction to your longing. While desire awakens the will to move, intention clarifies where that movement is headed *and what motivates it.*

Clear intention transforms a general want into a focused aim. It brings your desire into form, aligning it with deeper values, meaning, and purpose. It's not enough to want something—you must understand *why* you want it, *what is motivating you,* and whether that motivation is aligned with your true self or rooted in fear, conditioning, ego needs, or illusion.

This step invites you to uncover the driving motivation behind your desire. Is it born of soul truth or a need for approval? Is it calling you forward with integrity—or pushing from behind with pressure, fear, or fantasy? That clarity becomes your inner compass, helping you navigate distractions, resistance, or doubt. It steadies your course when the way forward becomes uncertain.

Not all intentions are conscious. Some are shaped by hidden fears, old identities, or driven by the ego. Clarifying your intention means listening deeply—not just to what you hope to gain, but to the motivations underneath. Sometimes hesitation reveals old patterns or fear of change; other times its wisdom asking you to pause and realign.

An intention rooted in genuine motivation resonates in the

body. It stirs emotional truth—excitement, reverence, calm determination. That feeling is your signal that the intention is *true*—that it's yours.

Think of this step as refining your internal compass by bringing your motivations into full awareness. The clearer your motivation, the more naturally your intention—and the energy behind it—will align your actions and choices.

Now, bring your desire from Lesson One back into your awareness—and begin to explore the *real motivation* behind it. This is your moment to listen within and let truth reveal itself.

Reflect & Clarify: Why Do I Want This?

Desire opens the door—but intention walks through it. These questions help me uncover the deeper motivations, beliefs, and emotional resonance behind my path. I look within and honestly write down my true motivations for wanting what I want.

My Deeper Motivation

- Why do I truly want this?
- Why does this feel meaningful or necessary in my life right now?
- Why do I believe this will bring something valuable or fulfilling?
- Why does this particular goal or dream keep returning to me?

My Connection to the Goal

- Why do I feel called to pursue this with my full energy?

- Why does this path feel real—or not fully real—within me?
- Why do I feel emotionally connected—or disconnected—from this intention?
- Why do I sense this is my true direction and not someone else's dream for me?

The Authenticity of My Motivation

- Why am I choosing this—because I believe in it or because I am seeking safety, approval, or validation?
- Why am I drawn to this vision—what part of me is speaking through it?
- Why do I feel a strong emotional reaction—joy, fear, doubt—when I picture this goal becoming real?
- Why has this intention surfaced now? What inner truth or desire is asking to be expressed?

Inner Dialogue & Uncovering Hidden Motivation

- Why do I hesitate when I imagine fully stepping into this goal?
- Why have I not already moved forward—and what may have held me back?
- Why do certain doubts or emotions arise when I think of this dream becoming reality?
- Why might part of me still question if I am truly ready or worthy to claim this?

Exercise: Clarifying Your Intention Through Creativity

Before committing to your intention, be sure it is truly your own—and that it serves not only your personal growth but also your environment and community.

Take time to clarify any doubts or past resistance that may

have held you back. What has kept you from moving forward until now? Gently explore these questions and begin to work through them.

Once you understand the emotions your desire stirs within you, give them creative expression. Celebrate your clarity—dance it, sketch it, sing it, write a poem, or make a collage.

If you encounter conflicting or resistant emotions, don't push them away. Instead, use them as fuel. Transform any inner tension or past difficulty into a new creation. Let the very obstacles that once blocked your path become stepping stones toward creative solutions.

A Closing Thought: Let Motivation Lead Intention

Clarity is not something we force—it's something we allow to emerge. As you reflect on your intention, let your true motivation rise from the stillness like a steady flame, not a spark that flickers in the wind.

When your *why* is real—when your motivation rings true—it becomes a compass. It doesn't shout, but it points the way with quiet certainty. It helps you walk through resistance, distraction, and confusion with your heart intact.

If your intention feels clouded, don't rush to name it. Sit with it. Let your deeper motivation come into view. Sometimes it arrives gently, as a whisper beneath the noise.

Sometimes it stirs you with unmistakable resonance.

And when it comes—when you feel the spark of purpose align with your desire—let that motivation shape your path forward. Speak it aloud. Write it down. Let it inform your choices, your energy, and your daily steps.

Let your intention become a living expression of your deepest motivation—not just a direction, but a devotion.

10

Lesson Three
THE POWER OF IMPECCABILITY AND VISION – A SYNERGISTIC APPROACH

There is a dance between discipline and inspiration, between the focused drive to act and the intuitive clarity that shows us where we're going. This lesson is about learning to harness both.

Impeccability is not perfectionism—it is a standard of inner alignment. It means showing up with integrity, consistency, and wholeheartedness. It asks: *Am I truly living in accordance with my intention?* It's the daily choice to follow through, to refine your efforts, and to stay attuned to what matters most.

It invites commitment without rigidity, action without overwhelm, structure without losing soul.

Vision, in contrast, is what fuels and guides impeccability. It gives form to your desire and direction to your effort. Vision asks you to *see* the outcome before it exists—to imagine it so vividly that it draws you forward. This is not daydreaming—it is a creative act of inner seeing that informs your outer doing.

When impeccability and vision work together, they generate a field of momentum and magnetism. One without the other becomes unbalanced—impeccability alone can become dry or mechanical; vision alone can remain floating and ungrounded. But in synergy, they build the bridge between intention and realization.

This lesson invites you to bring focused attention to your

path while keeping your inner eye on the horizon. Let your effort be infused with clarity, and your clarity supported by commitment.

~

Reflection & Practice: Living with Impeccability and Vision

To consciously shape your reality, you must align your thoughts, feelings, and actions with precision and integrity. Impeccability means staying true to your vision through consistent, focused effort—without slipping into rigidity or self-judgment. When you expect limitation, you meet limitation. When you expect success, you begin to move toward it.

Use the following reflections to deepen your relationship with both impeccability and vision. These questions are designed to bring greater awareness to the way you show up for your desire—and the version of yourself you are becoming.

Impeccability: Inner Discipline and Aligned Action

Mental Alignment: How Am I relating to This Desire?

- What happens —emotionally and physically—when I focus on my desired outcome?
- Am I taking consistent actions toward my desire? If not, where do I tend to lose focus or momentum— through distraction, uncertainty, resistance, or familiar habits?
- How do I respond when I consider finding and committing to a workable schedule, structure or program to support my goal? Do I feel energized, hesitant, overwhelmed?
- How easily do I get pulled off track? Do I notice

myself drifting into avoidance, indecision, or delay
when planning or engaging with this project?
- Have I already begun creating a schedule, plan, or
routine that helps me take concrete steps forward? If
not, how do I feel about setting one up now? ... Do I
sense enthusiasm, resistance, fear, or a tendency to
postpone?

Commitment in Action: Honoring the Path Forward

- Looking at my life now, is there one action I can
commit to with full presence and integrity... with
impeccability?
- As I consider this commitment, what sensations or
emotions arise— mentally, emotionally, or physically?
How might this ripple out into the world around me?
- Am I still willing to proceed with my commitment?
- How might I carry it out in a sustainable way?
  - What approach feels most natural or effective?
  - How long am I willing to stay with it?
  - How will I know when it's time to reassess or
evolve?

Vision: Seeing, Feeling, and Embodying the New Reality

- How vividly can I imagine the reality that would
unfold if this desire came fully to life? Can I see it, feel
it, and begin to embody it as if it were already true?
- Am I giving myself permission to truly feel this
possibility—to experience the joy, fulfillment, and
empowerment that it brings?
- How rich and detailed is the vision I'm holding? Can
I bring in more texture, emotion, and sensory
aliveness?

- How naturally can I begin to live as if this new reality is already here?
- How would I speak, move, or choose from within that version of myself?
- How does it feel when I truly inhabit this vision and act from that place?

Creative Integration: Rehearsing Your Reality

Use the power of your imagination to create and strengthen your vision. Your subconscious mind responds to what you consistently focus on—whether real or imagined.

Let your mind rehearse this future not as a wish, but as a lived experience.

- Can I see myself thriving within the new reality I'm envisioning?
- What qualities would I need to embody in order to fully live this reality?
- Am I open to evolving my thoughts, attitudes or behaviors to align with this vision?
- How might I shift from imagining to inhabiting this reality more fully each day?
- Is my vision board still aligned with my current desire? Do I feel called to add, remove, or refine any images, words, or colors. to reflect my current resonance?
- When I look at my vision board, does it rekindle the fire of my desire and reaffirm my commitment to walk this path with integrity and inspiration?
- If it doesn't, refresh your vision board to reflect what feels most alive and true for you now.

Create your own affirmations rooted in your desire and intention. Begin with the phrase: "It is my intention to..."

Let your words be simple, sincere, and energizing—a clear reflection of your commitment.

Speak your affirmations aloud each day to strengthen your focus and align your energy. Let them remind you of what truly matters and the path you've chosen to walk.

Examples:

- It is my intention to bring excellence into all that I do.
- It is my intention to love and receive love in all that I do.
- It is my intention to live a life aligned with my deepest values.
- It is my intention to act courageously towards the realization of my dream.

Closing Thought: Impeccability is the engine. Vision is the map.

As you align your actions with your higher vision, the path of Excellence becomes not something you follow, but something you embody—moment by moment, choice by choice. You're not just pursuing a dream. You are becoming the clearest, truest version of yourself— grounded in integrity, guided by clarity, and alive with purpose.

11

Lesson Four
THE ART OF MANIFESTING WITH GRACE

Elegance - The Flow of Effortless Excellence

There is a way of creating that doesn't strain, struggle, or force. It moves like a dancer in rhythm with life—graceful, intentional, and attuned.

This is the way of **Elegance**.

To embody elegance is to know when to act and when to allow. It's choosing precision over excess, presence over pressure. It is the path of refinement—where power meets ease.

Elegance doesn't mean passivity. It means trusting your rhythm, aligning your inner world with outer action, and honoring *beauty* as much as *results*. It is the *art of doing less and becoming more*—not by holding back, but by letting go of struggle.

It's also the art of sustainability—moving forward in a way that energizes, not exhausts you. When you live in harmony with your intention, synchronicities arise, and the next steps often reveal themselves with grace.

And like all great art, elegance is cultivated.

Take your time with this step. Not every reflection may apply directly to your process right now—choose the ones that feel most resonant. Let them gently guide your attention toward flow, balance, and refinement.

Mental Alignment: Am I Inviting Flow or Forcing It?

- Explore the tone and texture of your current path. Gently observe your inner landscape.
- How do I move through life—gracefully and in sync with the moment, or through effort and pressure?
- How much of my current effort is truly necessary? Where could I allow more space and softness?
- When something comes easily, do I welcome it fully— or do I feel I must earn everything through hard work?
- Can I trust life to support me even when I'm not trying to control every outcome?

Releasing the Need for Struggle: What Beliefs Am I Holding?

Struggle can be familiar—but is it essential? Let's question that story.

- How familiar or comfortable am I with struggle as a way of life?
- Have I associated success with sacrifice and hardship?
- Do I secretly believe that if it's easy, it's not meaningful?
- What would shift in my life if I welcomed ease as a natural part of my path?

Attuning to the Journey: Is My Desire Aligned with Elegance?

Bring your attention back to your current desire.

- How much ease am I allowing in this journey?
- Are synchronicities showing up—or am I pushing against resistance?
- Am I feeling frustrated or disheartened by a lack of progress?
- What would it feel like to trust the process more deeply?

Deepening the Practice: Self-Love, Receiving, and the Principle of Least Effort

- Do I love myself enough to let things come easily—to know I deserve this ease?
- Am I willing to accomplish more by doing less?
- Where might I simplify, soften, or let go?

Elegance is self-love in motion. It's the willingness to be nourished by your own efforts—not drained by them.

Embodying Elegance: A Movement Meditation

Elegance is not only a concept—it's a **felt experience**.

Try one of these simple practices to let your body lead the way:

Option 1 - Walking the Figure Eight

- Place two crystals or stones on the floor about a meter apart.
- Stand between them, centering your awareness.

- Imagine a figure 8, with each loop around one stone.
- Slowly begin to walk this pattern for 5–7 minutes.
- Stay present with your desire, intention, and vision—inviting them to move with ease and elegance.

Option 2 - Drawing the Figure Eight

- On a piece of paper, draw a continuous figure 8.
- Trace it with your finger for several minutes.
- Let your thoughts slow. Let your energy soften.
- Feel the rhythm of balance, the union of action and surrender.

A Closing Thought

Elegance is not about doing more—it's about becoming more aligned.

When you release the belief that struggle equals worthiness, you make space for life to meet you with grace. You begin to trust that beauty and ease are not luxuries, but signposts of alignment.

Let Elegance guide you like a river following its course—not hurried, not hesitant, but steady and sure. Move with intention, choose with care, and let each step be infused with meaning rather than effort.

In this space of flow, your desire ripens naturally. Your intention becomes magnetic. Your presence becomes powerful. You begin to co-create with life—not by controlling it, but by dancing with it.

Let Elegance become the signature of your path: Refined. Fluid. True.

12

Lesson Five
THE DANCE OF COURAGE AND JOY

Stepping Forward with Heart

There comes a moment in every journey when the path asks more of us—not more effort, but more heart. That moment is a doorway. To step through it is to choose **Courage**.

Courage doesn't mean the absence of fear. It's the willingness to feel fear, doubt, and uncertainty—and move forward anyway. It's staying connected to your desire, your vision, your truth, even when the way is unclear.

Courage means daring to act without guarantees. To keep showing up. To trust yourself enough to take the next step, even if it's a small one. It's not always loud.

Sometimes, it's a quiet breath and a whispered "yes" in the face of resistance.

And if courage is the step, **Joy** is the companion.

Joy is the energy that lifts your journey from duty to devotion. It renews your spirit, celebrates your growth, and reconnects you with your essence. It reminds you that this path is not only about becoming—it's about enjoying the becoming.

To walk with both Courage and Joy is to meet life open-heartedly—embracing the mess, the mystery, and the magic.

Let this lesson be your invitation to lean in—bravely, playfully, and wholeheartedly.

Reflect: What Does Courage Ask of You Now?

- What am I afraid of as I pursue this desire or project?
- What part of this journey feels uncertain, risky, or vulnerable?
- Am I waiting until I feel "ready"? What might happen if I acted now?
- What decision or action have I been avoiding— and why?
- Can I trust that I have the strength to handle whatever comes?

Courage isn't the absence of fear—it's the decision to move forward anyway.

Micro-Movement: A Small, Brave Step

- What is one courageous action I could take this week? (Something real. Something that nudges you forward.)
- What would help me follow through? (Support? Preparation? A promise to myself?)
- If I'm not ready to act yet—what would help me get ready?

Choose one act of courage—name it, honor it, and make a promise to follow through.

Reclaiming Courage from the Past

Sometimes we forget how often we've already been brave.

- Recall a time when you acted with courage.
- What fear did you face? What helped you move forward?
- What did you learn from that experience?
- How can that memory strengthen you now?

Joy: The Soul's Way of Saying Yes

Joy is more than happiness—it's aliveness, wholeness and a return to yourself. It is also an act of courage—to let yourself feel good, to celebrate, to receive.

- Do I allow myself to feel joy as I make progress?
- Do I withhold celebration until I've "earned it" or reached the end?
- Where in my life do I resist pleasure or ease?
- What brings me simple joy—and am I making space for it?

Let joy be fuel, not just a reward.

Reconnect with Joy through Preference

Your preferences are sacred clues to your joy. Honoring them is a quiet act of courage.

- Can I clearly distinguish between a need and a preference?
- Do I give myself permission to follow my preferences?
- Where might I still hold back out of guilt, fear of judgment, or habit?

- What would change if I honored what truly lights me up?

Practice: The Courage-Joy Connection

Let these two powers walk hand in hand, each one strengthening the other.

1. Name the action. What is one courageous move I feel called to take?
2. Name the fear. If fear is present, can I name it gently, without judgment?
3. Listen with compassion. What is this fear asking for—more time, greater safety, reassurance? How can I tend to it, listen to it, befriend it, and help it soften?
4. Honor the journey. Document this process—both the action and the emotions that arise. This, too, is part of the path. The real journey is not the result, but how I meet each step along the way.
5. Envision the joy. Even if I'm not ready to act, can I imagine what might unfold? Can I feel the joy waiting on the other side of courage?

Journal Prompts

- What brave step am I ready to take this week?
- What resistance do I feel—and what do I need to move through it?
- What joy might arise from following through?
- Where in my body do I feel joy—could I return there when I need courage?
- How do I want to celebrate my small (or big) victories?
- What message does Joy have for me right now?

A Closing Thought

Courage doesn't wait for certainty. And joy isn't only waiting at the finish line. Let them walk with you now—one step, one breath, one brave, joyful yes at a time.

13

Lesson Six

THE ALCHEMY OF UNDERSTANDING AND WISDOM

Where Knowledge Meets Insight

There are moments on the path when desire, intention, and vision begin to take shape.

You know what you want—and you're willing to move toward it.

But how?

This is where Understanding steps in—bringing structure to inspiration, clarity to confusion, and direction to desire.

Understanding maps the terrain, breaks complexity into steps, and steadies the mind with tangible next actions. It satisfies our need to know—to comprehend the path ahead.

Yet, understanding alone is not enough.

To walk the path with depth and integrity, you must invite Wisdom.

Wisdom listens not only to the mind but to the heart, the gut, the soul.

It's the quiet voice that says, *"This is the right time"*—or *"Wait."*

It sees beyond the obvious, aligning your efforts with a greater harmony.

Together, understanding and wisdom form an alchemy: head and heart, strategy and soul, clarity and compassion.

Let this lesson be an invitation to integrate both—to make your efforts not only efficient, but meaningful.

Understanding: Reflecting on What You've Gained

- How much understanding have I achieved in the process of exploring and pursuing my desire?
- How much intellectual clarity do I now have about the steps needed to achieve it?
- Have I acquired the necessary knowledge and information related to my goal?
- Has my understanding of the process helped me create a roadmap to guide my efforts?
- Has understanding supported me in breaking the vision into manageable steps and forming a strategic plan?

Learning and Growth: What Might Still Be Needed.

- Do I need to study further, research more, or seek out other learning opportunities to deepen my understanding?
- Are there specific skills, tools, or resources that would strengthen my foundation?
- Who or what could support me as I refine my approach?

Recognizing Obstacles.

- What might be blocking me from doing the action(s) necessary to pursue my objective?
- What emotion is triggered by this process and how can I handle it constructively, with creativity and compassion?

Problem-Solving and Application

- Has my understanding helped me overcome obstacles or challenges along the way?
- Has it helped me identify solutions or alternative paths forward?
- Did my growing clarity improve my ability to communicate my vision and collaborate with others?

Wisdom: Recognizing the Deeper Guidance

- Have I been able to connect with my inner wisdom— seeing the bigger picture and deeper truths behind my process?
- Has wisdom helped me integrate knowledge with a deeper sense of intuition?
- Can I recall a particular moment when I tapped into a deeper understanding coming from a place beyond logical reasoning? A moment that balanced analytical thinking with emotional and spiritual insights?

Alignment with Purpose

- Has wisdom complemented my understanding by offering deeper, intuitive insight that guided me forward?

- Has my original vision evolved with wisdom ensuring a deeper alignment with my values, ethics and higher purpose?

A Closing Thought

Understanding brings direction. Wisdom brings meaning. Together, they create a life not just of success—but of depth, harmony, and grace.

Let this be the moment where your clarity meets your truth—and from their union, a new way forward begins.

14

Lesson Seven
THE ART OF EXCELLENCE

The Integration of All That You Are

There is a moment, after the striving, the learning, the refining—when something clicks.

A quiet sense of knowing fills you.

You've given your best, not out of force, but from alignment.

And something beautiful has emerged.

Not just a result, but a way of being.

That is Excellence.

It is not perfection.

It is wholeness in motion.

It is your desire, your intention, your impeccability, your vision— carried forth with elegance, courage, joy, understanding, and wisdom.

Excellence isn't an act.

It's a resonance.

Excellence is the natural culmination of the journey you've taken—the harmonious integration of desire, intention, impeccability, vision, elegance, courage, joy, understanding, and wisdom. It is not a separate goal, but the flowering of all that you have cultivated along the way.

To live with excellence is to strive for the highest standards in all that you do—not from pressure or perfectionism, but from the quiet knowing that you are capable of your best. It is about quality, integrity, and presence—whether you are launching a business, tending a relationship, or simply choosing how to meet the day.

Excellence asks for attention to detail. For grace and consistency. For a commitment to doing things not just well, but beautifully, ethically, and sustainably.

It is a mindset of continuous refinement—an invitation to stretch without burning out, to rise without losing balance, to create impact while honoring your values.

And when excellence is reached, it brings with it joy. A sense of fulfillment. The deep satisfaction of knowing you gave your best. It inspires others. It endures.

Let this lesson be both a celebration and a continuation—an honoring of what you've achieved, and a gentle reminder that excellence is not a final destination, but a way of being.

A daily practice. A legacy in the making.

Exercises for Excellence: Bringing it All Together

You've walked through each step with presence, courage, and intention. Now it's time to pause and reflect--to trace the arc of your journey and honor what has shifted within you.

1. Desires — Revisit My Longings
   - What desires were present in me at the beginning of this journey?
   - Which ones remain? Have any transformed or clarified?
   - Has anything changed, softened, deepened?
2. Clear Intention — Clarify Focus
   - How clear was I when I began—could I see the "why" behind my desire?

- ○ Has my purpose remained steady—or
    transformed along the way?
3. Impeccability and Vision — Reflect on Integrity and
   Guidance
   - ○ Have my steps been aligned with my words, my
     vision, my integrity?
   - ○ In what ways did I embody impeccability in
     thought, word, and action?
   - ○ How did my original vision support and
     guide me?
   - ○ Did my vision remain steady, or did it evolve?
   - ○ What role did vision play in my journey?
4. Elegance — Move with Grace
   - ○ How gracefully did I allow life to support my
     unfolding?
   - ○ Did I create space for flow, ease, or synchronicity?
   - ○ Where did I experience struggle or resistance—
     and how did I return to elegance?
5. Courage and Joy — Face My Fears and Celebrate
   Moments with Joy
   - ○ What challenges did I face that required courage?
   - ○ Did I take brave actions —even when I was
     unsure?
   - ○ What fears emerged—and how did I move
     through them?
   - ○ Where did joy surprise me? Sustain me? Invite me
     to keep going?
   - ○ Did I celebrate my progress, both big and small?
6. Understanding and Wisdom
   - ○ What understanding did I gain—about my goal,
     my process, or myself?
   - ○ How did my intellect support me—or limit me—
     along the way?
   - ○ What truth did my deeper knowing reveal?
   - ○ What moments felt like wisdom beyond logic?

- How did synchronicity or inner knowing shape my path?

7. Excellence — Recognize What I've Become
   - What does excellence look and feel like in this moment?
   - Can I see how this process is repeatable in other areas of life?
   - How might I carry this way of being into what comes next?

Practice: Anchor the Experience of Excellence

- Choose a quiet moment.
- Light a candle.
- Breathe deeply and slowly for a few minutes.
- Notice what happens.
- Does your body relax? Does your thinking slow down?
- How does your body feel?
- Bring your awareness upon your Excellence process.
- Acknowledge that you have walked a path of devotion to your self.
- You have felt, thought, listened, acted, risked, refined.
- You can now see the beauty you've created through care and consciousness.
- Experience the resonance of excellence—not flawlessly, but simply, truthfully.
- Let it settle. Let it root.

Replication: Excellence as a Life Practice

Now that you know the process:

- Will you let this experience guide your future steps?

- Will you remember to return to these steps whenever you feel off-track?
- Will you allow yourself to bring this level of integrity and presence to other areas of your life?
- Will you allow what you've learned to be real, simply by embodying it?

Excellence is not something you chase. It's not a destination. It's something you choose to *become*.

Final Reflection Questions

- What part of this journey surprised me the most?
- Where did I stretch beyond what I believed was possible?
- What am I most proud of?

And finally:

- How will I carry excellence forward into my next creation?

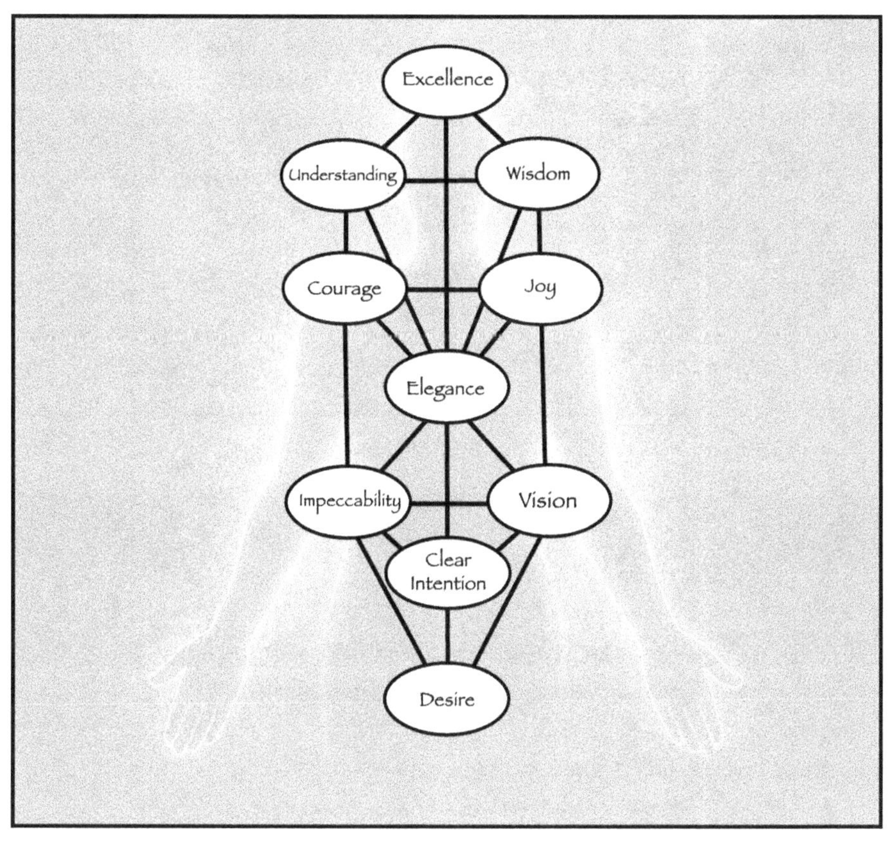

Excellence
Understanding
Wisdom
Courage
Joy
Elegance
Impeccability
Vision
Clear
Intention
Desire

Epilogue

There is no final arrival.

*Only the next step—taken with a little more aware-
ness, a little more joy, and a little more trust.*

*This journey you have walked—through desire,
intention, impeccability, vision, elegance,
courage, joy, understanding, and wisdom—has
not led you somewhere outside yourself.*

*It has brought you home. To the part of you that
remembers.*

*Excellence is not a performance. It's a way of listen-
ing. Of aligning. Of saying yes to what is most
essential in you—again and again.*

Let your life become the teacher now.

*Let the steps you take speak the truth of who you are
becoming.*

*And when you forget—because we all do—return to
the spark, the desire, the call that brought you
here.*

*I am walking this path too. Still learning. Still
refining. Still falling in love with the Mystery
that guides us all.*

I trust you.

I celebrate you.

*And I thank you—for the excellence you are becom-
ing, and the light you are leaving behind.*

With all my heart,
Shama

BACK BOOK COVER

This book provides a clear pathway: a transformative journey through Seven Steps that take us to Excellence. These steps are designed to help us align our choices, intentions and actions, with our highest potential. Together, they form a roadmap for creating a life of purpose and integrity while nurturing our personal growth. Each chapter explores one of these steps, weaving together Shama's personal stories and insights to help us embrace and integrate these principles into our lives.

Shama Viola (Manuela Terraluna) was born in Ravenna, Italy, and moved to the United States at age 24 in search of greater personal freedom and self-expression. Over the next three decades, she lived in California and Hawaii, studying with many gifted teachers and becoming a respected spiritual mentor in her own right. In 2001, her journey led her back to Italy, where she became a citizen of Damanhur—an intentional spiritual community renowned for its underground Temple of Humankind and its pioneering exploration of consciousness, sacred ritual, and human potential.

A lifelong seeker and guide, Shama has traveled extensively, offering courses, presentations, and transformational journeys that invite others to awaken their potential and walk a path of integrity, sacredness, and joy. Her teachings reflect a deep commitment to the path of Excellence—not as perfection, but as the ongoing refinement of one's soul and purpose.

She is the creator of Bral Talej, an intuitive oracle deck rooted in Damanhur's sacred language, and the author of its companion guidebook. Through her natural gift of intuition, she offers personal readings and courses on how to use the deck as a tool for inner guidance and spiritual insight.